TREASURES
of VERY RARE
Depression Glass

IDENTIFICATION
AND VALUE GUIDE

Gene Florence

COLLECTOR BOOKS
A Division of Schroeder Publishing Co., Inc.

Front cover: Left, Diane pitcher, $250.00; right top, Peacock & Wild Rose fan vase, $395.00; right center, large Ultramarine reamer, $1,250.00; right bottom, Candlewick candy and lid, $900.00.

Back cover: Background, Dogwood cake plate, $165.00; left, "Philbe," Fire-King cookie jar, $1,500.00; center, American Pioneer candlestick, $125.00; right, Sandwich juice pitcher, $395.00.

Cover design by Beth Summers
Book design by Karen Geary and Kelly Dowdy

COLLECTOR BOOKS
P.O. Box 3009
Paducah, Kentucky 42002-3009

www.collectorbooks.com
or
Gene Florence
P.O. Box 22186
Lexington, KY 40522
or
P.O. Box 64
Astatula, FL 34705

www.geneflorence.com

Copyright © 2003 Gene Florence

The current values in this book should be used only as a guide. They are not intended to set prices, which vary from one section of the country to another. Auction prices as well as dealer prices vary greatly and are affected by condition as well as demand. Neither the author nor the publisher assumes responsibility for any losses that might be incurred as a result of consulting this guide.

Searching For A Publisher?

We are always looking for people knowledgeable within their fields. If you feel that there is a real need for a book on your collectible subject and have a large comprehensive collection, contact Collector Books.

Acknowledgments

The concept for this compilation book was my former editor at Collector Books, Lisa Stroup's, who felt so many "new-to-glass" people were missing opportunities to know the really rare pieces shown in long out-of-print works. Since inception, a great many obstacles have been overcome to bring you a phenomenal 368 pages of glassware you may never see anyplace else! However, should you find a piece; you will now know to latch onto it as the unusual piece it is.

I owe a particular debt of gratitude to Dick and Pat Spencer and Lynn Welker for their patience in helping acquire and price many of the rarities pictured throughout this book. Dick and Pat have borrowed and transported glassware for me to photograph at the studio many times. Their reward is sharing their love of glass with collectors, as there is no way I could ever pay them enough to make it worth all their trouble and time. Lynn has lent me his personal rarities of Cambridge glass as well as arranged for me to borrow glassware from the Cambridge museum, which if you have an opportunity to visit in Cambridge, Ohio, you should.

In addition, I have had tremendous help from collectors and dealers in obtaining pieces shown. Without them, one person could have never have amassed enough rarely seen items to finish six editions of *Very Rare Glassware of the Depression Era*. In order to make sure no one is left out, I am attempting to list all those who lent glassware for past rare books as well as this one. Some of the glass lent will not be represented in this book due to space limitations, but please know I thank all those involved. (I hope we have remembered everyone who has been a part of all these Herculean undertakings over the years.) Everyone in glass owes our gratitude to these kind people for their assistance in advancing the field of knowledge for our particular glassware.

Bill and Barbara Adt
Molly Allen
Anchor Hocking Glass Corp.
Robert and Betty Bacon
Dennis Bailek
Martha Beals
Jack Bell
Bettie's Cupboard/Orphan Annie's
John and Judy Bines
Parke and Joyce Bloyer
Ann Brady
The Cambridge Glass Museum
Clarence Clark
Gary and Sue Clark
Sam and Becky Collings
Bob and Nancy Cosner
Hester Davis
Sally Davis
John and Trannie Davis
Carrie Domitz
Ruth Donnell
Bill and Millie Downey
Victor Elliot
Myra Evans
Cathy Florence
Chad Florence
Marc Florence
Rosemary Gary
Ed Goshe

Leslie Hansen
Austin and Shirley Hartsock
Gary Ackerman and Larry Harvey
Jim and Wilda Heft
Yvonne Heil
Geogeann Henry
Sandy Hilterbran
Earl and Beverly Hines
Steve Howard
Roy and Doris Isaccs
Marianne Jackson
Ted and Judy Johnson
Jim and Helen Kennon
Kevin and Barbara Kiley
Jim and Dot Kimball
Lorrie Kitchen
Dorothy Klosterman
Darlene Kouri
John and Evelyn Knowles
Dan Kramer
Virgil and Joyce Krug
Charles Larsen
Swede and Kay Larsson
Bruce Leslie
Ralph and Fran Leslie
Michael and Anna Lukasik
Nancy Maben
Ron and Barbara Marks
Frank and Sherry McClain

Terry and Celia McDuffee
Charles and Peggy McIntosh
Max Miller
Jackie Morgan
Morris Antiques
Steve Nadort
John Peterson
Lottie Porter
Beckye Richardson
Dr. Bob and Judy Schmidgalt
George and Veronica Sionakides
Iris Slayton
Bill and Phyllis Smith
Joe and Florence Solito
Katie Spriggs
Paul and Debbie Torsiello
Dan and Geri Tucker
David and Sarah Vandalsem
Ronnie Marshall Vickers
Dean and Mary Watkins
Harold and Susan Watson
Keith and Jane White
Kenn and Margaret Whitmyer
Babara Wolfe
Mrs. Harold Workman
Michael and Leegh Wyse
Delmer Youngen

Introduction

After six editions of *Very Rare Glassware of the Depression Era* were issued there became an issue of its marketability to novice collectors; so it was decided to put that series to rest. Since then, however, there have been a multitude of requests asking when another was being released or how could out-of-print editions be obtained. Therefore, as a happy median, the publisher decided on a more complete book, using some photos from the earlier books with additional photos never before seen. Not all pieces were repeated, as some items turned out to be more common over the years than previously known, and some previous photos were unavailable to reuse these many years later. Since we want to show you the best photos possible, some pieces had to be omitted as not being up to today's standards.

Most items shown are rarely seen, and a few are even experimental prototypes or specially designed for a particular person by a factory worker. Some items will never again be found in the open market or may only appear when a collection is sold or released into the market for some reason such as death or divorce. Some items pictured were never officially issued for consumers. We have examples only because they remain in glass company morgues (a retirement place for experimental designs and colors of their glassware). The good news is that should you uncover one of these special pieces, you will know there is a ready market for it.

This book is arranged by pattern name rather than by glass company as were the original books. Thus, you can search for the rarities in your pattern easily. Be sure to study them all, lest you miss a bargain! Even if you do not collect all patterns, you need to be aware that rarely found items in other patterns will make great trade or sell items for whatever you wish to pursue.

Rarity, as defined by this book, means rarely seen or for sale at any price. Prices listed are from owners' evaluations. Many pieces remain in collections today and have not been on the open market for years. Some rarely found items are difficult to sell due to extremely high prices. It is easier to sell one hundred pieces for $100 each than it is to sell one piece for $10,000. Many collectors have $100, but few have $10,000 for a piece of glass. Then, too, there are pieces selling for $1000 or more that are not really as rare as they are desirable. As an illustration, demand for Mayfair pink sugar lids or pink Sharon cheese dishes keeps those prices high, but they are not really so rare as just wanted by enough collectors to keep the price on an upward trend.

Some of the rarities in this book have less than a dozen known examples; some may approach fifty or more. Yes, there is still a chance for you to find one! It's amazing what still turns up in the market. For instance, one collector in Florida was in a shop right before closing time a few years ago. When she arrived home, my rare book showing a Cambridge Cleo temple jar was in her mail box. When she saw that jar, she remembered seeing one in the shop she was visiting that afternoon. Since that piece had been priced about 10% of the price in my book, she took the morning off from work and was waiting at the door when the shop opened the next day. She thanked me profusely at a show a few weeks later as she would never have known the value or rarity otherwise.

Adam-Sierra
Butter dish, pink, Jeannette Glass Co.
$1,800.00.

Albemarle
Footed sodas (left) and sherbets (right), experimental blue, each 5 ounce, A. H. Heisey & Co.
Sodas $400.00 each; sherbets $400.00 each.

American
Dresser set, Fostoria.
$400.00.

American
Pitcher and tumblers, green, Fostoria.
Pitcher, $1,500.00; tumblers $200.00 each.

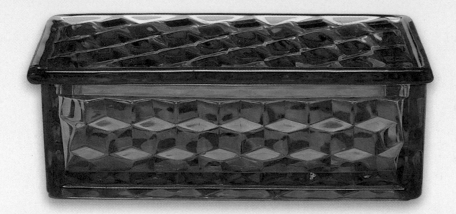

American
Hankerchief box, blue,
Fostoria.
$1,500.00.

American
Rectangular pin tray, blue,
Fostoria.
$300.00.

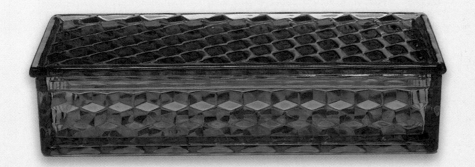

American
Glove box, blue,
Fostoria.
$1,500.00.

American
Rectangular dresser tray, blue, 10", Fostoria.
$300.00.

American
Puff box, blue, Fostoria.
$950.00.

American
Handled tea, handled sherbet, and soap dish, crystal, Fostoria.
Handled tea, $400.00; handled sherbet, $125.00; soap dish, $3,000.00.

American
Hexagonal sugar and creamer, crystal, Fostoria.
Sugar, $350.00; creamer, $350.00.

American
Comport, crystal, Fostoria.
$495.00.

American
Banana split dish (right) and
chocolate box (left), crystal,
Fostoria. Banana split dish,
$595.00; chocolate box,
$250.00.

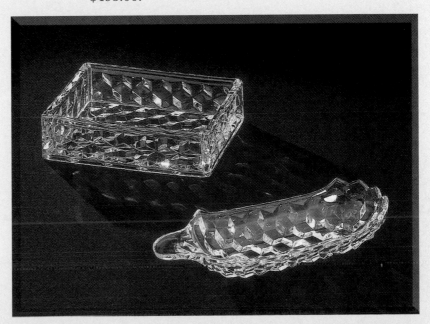

American
Bowl and pitcher, crystal,
Fostoria.
$2,250.00 each.

American
Basket, crystal,
Fostoria.
$750.00.

American
Whimsey vase made from tumbler,
crystal, Fostoria.
$250.00.

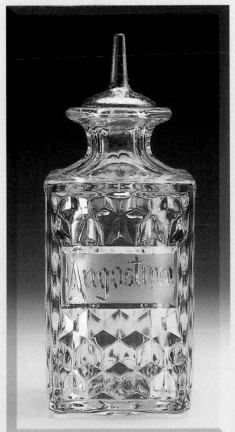

American
Angostura bitters bottle,
crystal, Fostoria.
$80.00.

American
Orange bitters bottle, Fostoria.
$80.00.

American
Crush fruit, crystal, Fostoria.
$2,000.00.

American
Footed tumbler, opaque blue-green,
Fostoria.
$150.00.

American
Footed tumbler, opaque white speckled,
Fostoria.
$150.00.

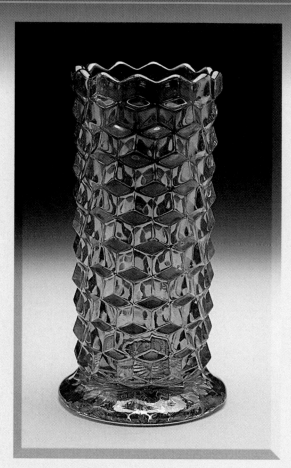

American
Vase, iridescent, 8", Fostoria.
$275.00.

American
Vase, milk blue, Fostoria.
$75.00.

American
Covered box, crystal, Fostoria.
$795.00.

American
Bowl, opaque blue, 6", Fostoria.
$125.00.

American
Sponge dish, 6½" with drain insert,
Fostoria.
$975.00.

American
Flower pot with perforated cover, crystal, Fostoria.
$2,000.00.

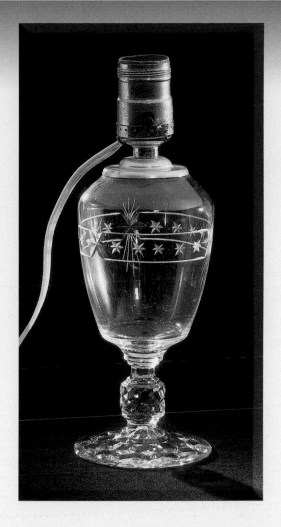

"American Lady"
Lamp, crystal, Fostoria.
$195.00.

American Pioneer
Candlestick, amber, 6½", Liberty Glass Works.
$125.00.

American Pioneer
Covered urns, amber, Liberty Glass Works.
5" covered urn, $250.00; 7" covered urn, $275.00.

American Sweetheart
Console bowl, cobalt blue, 18", MacBeth-Evans Glass Co.
$1,500.00.

American Sweetheart
Creamer and sugar, metallic finish applied over cobalt,
MacBeth-Evans Glass Co.
$225.00 each.

American Sweetheart
Miniature console bowl, 6½",
MacBeth-Evans Glass Co.
$2,000.00.

American Sweetheart
Dinner plate, crystal,
MacBeth-Evans Glass Co.
$50.00.

American Sweetheart
Cream soup, crystal,
MacBeth-Evans Glass Co.
$125.00.

American Sweetheart
Sugar with two styles of lids, Monax, MacBeth-Evans Glass Co.
Sugar, $8.00; lids, $500.00 each.

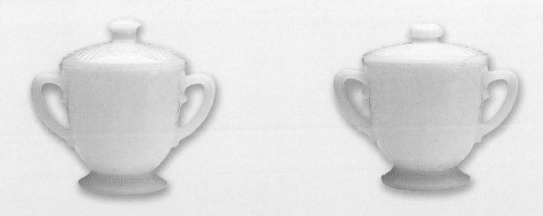

American Sweetheart
Two-handled consommé, Monax, 4", MacBeth-Evans Glass Co.
$250.00.

American Sweetheart
Berry bowl, smoke, 9", MacBeth-Evans Glass Co.
$275.00.

Anniversary
Cake plate (front and back), shell
pink, Jeannette Glass Co.
$395.00.

Apple Blossom with Rosalie
Handled serving tray, Emerald green, 12", Cambridge Glass Co.
$250.00.

Apple Blossom
#1341 mushroom cordial, amber,
Cambridge Glass Co.
$65.00.

Apple Blossom
#3400/78 cocktail shaker, amber,
38 ounce,
Cambridge Glass Co.
$350.00.

Apple Blossom
#1066 sham bottom tumbler, amber,
12 ounce, Cambridge Glass Co.
$75.00.

Apple Blossom
Handled plate, amethyst with
silver decoration,
Cambridge Glass Co.
$125.00.

Apple Blossom
#193 oil bottle, blue, 6 ounce,
Cambridge Glass Co.
$750.00.

Apple Blossom
#3135 cordial, blue, 4", Cambridge Glass Co.
$325.00.

Apple Blossom
Ice bucket, blue,
Cambridge Glass Co.
$350.00.

Apple Blossom
Pitcher, cobalt with silver,
Cambridge Glass Co.
$2,500.00.

Apple Blossom
#1402/94 Tally-Ho celery, Willow blue, 12", Cambridge Glass Co.
$295.00.

Apple Blossom
Sugar shaker, green,
Cambridge Glass Co.
$600.00.

Apple Blossom
Vase, ebony with platinum decoration,
Cambridge Glass Co.
$300.00.

Apple Blossom
#3400/96 oil and vinegar set, Heatherbloom, Cambridge Glass Co.
$600.00 set.

Apple Blossom
#3400 butter dish, Peach-Blo,
Cambridge Glass Co.
$395.00.

Apple Blossom
#3400/83 after-dinner cup and
square saucer, Willow blue,
Cambridge Glass Co.
$250.00.

Apple Blossom
#3400/40 sugar shaker, Peach-Blo,
Cambridge Glass Co.
$600.00.

"Avocado"
Pitcher (left) and tumbler (bottom),
white, Indiana Glass Co.
Pitcher $300.00; tumber $50.00.

Baroque
Three-light candlestick, amber (right) and
green (below), Fostoria Glass Co.
Amber $75.00; green $125.00.

Baroque
Flared bowl, pink, 12",
Fostoria Glass Co.
$250.00.

Black Forest
Ice tub, blue, Paden City Glass Co.
$1,000.00.

Black Forest
Cracker plate, Largo line 220, crystal, 10", Paden City Glass Co.
$90.00.

Black Forest
Tumble-up set, green,
Paden City Glass Co.
$695.00.

Black Forest
Five-part relish, green, 10½", Paden City Glass Co.
$500.00.

Black Forest
Pitcher, gold encrusted cobalt,
Paden City Glass Co.
$1,500.00.

Black Forest
Pitcher, pink, 10½", 72 ounce,
Paden City Glass Co.
$450.00.

Black Forest
Pitcher, pink, 8", 62 ounce,
Paden City Glass Co.
$500.00.

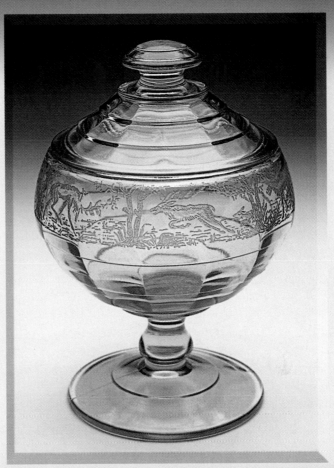

Black Forest
Candy dish, pink,
Paden City Glass Co.
$250.00.

Block Optic
Wine goblet, green, 3½",
Hocking Glass Co.
$500.00.

Block Optic
Juice pitcher, pink, Hocking Glass Co.
$950.00.

Block Optic
Grill plate, yellow, Hocking Glass Co.
$125.00.

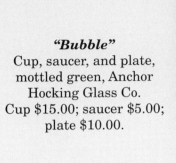

"Bubble"
Cup, saucer, and plate,
mottled green, Anchor
Hocking Glass Co.
Cup $15.00; saucer $5.00;
plate $10.00.

"Bubble"
Group shot, irridescent, Anchor Hocking Glass Co.
Dinner, $35.00; soup, $40.00; cup, $20.00; saucer, $5.00; salad plate, $20.00.

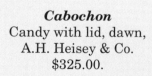

"Bubble"
Cup and saucer, pink,
Anchor Hocking
Glass Co.
$150.00.

Cabochon
Candy with lid, dawn,
A.H. Heisey & Co.
$325.00.

Cameo
Ice bucket, crystal,
Hocking Glass Co.
$450.00.

Cameo
Cocktail shaker, crystal,
Hocking Glass Co.
$995.00.

Cameo
Butter dish, yellow, Hocking Glass Co.
$1,500.00.

Cameo
Wine goblet, pink, 3½",
Hocking Glass Co.
$750.00.

Cameo
Milk pitcher, yellow,
Hocking Glass Co.
$2,000.00.

Cameo
Sandwich server, green,
Hocking Glass Co.
$7,250.00.

Cameo
Lamp base, green, Hocking Glass Co.
$1,000.00.

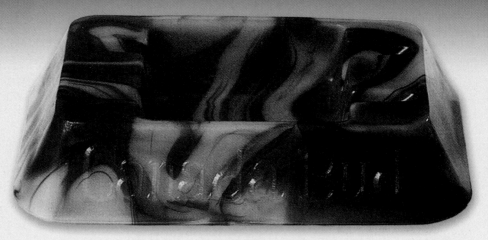

Canada Bud
Ashtray, Akro Agate Co.
$500.00.

Candlelight
#3114 cut cordial, crystal,
Cambridge Glass Co.
$350.00.

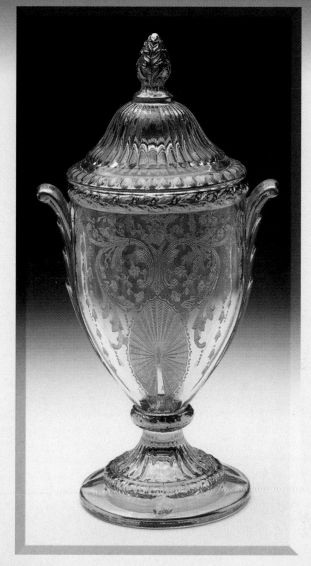

Candlelight
Urn, gold-encrusted crystal, 10",
Cambridge Glass Co.
$600.00.

Candlewick
Sherbet, Ritz blue,
Imperial Glass Co.
$100.00.

Candlewick
Oyster cocktail, Ritz blue,
Imperial Glass Co.
$125.00.

Candlewick
#400/268 two-part relish, caramel slag, 8", Imperial Glass Co.
$325.00.

Candlewick
Boudoir clock, crystal, 4", Imperial Glass Co.
$295.00.

Candlewick
#400/116 footed shaker, crystal,
Imperial Glass Co.
$70.00.

Candlewick
#400/125A divided oval bowl, crystal, 11", Imperial Glass Co.
$325.00.

Candlewick
#400/655 jar tower, Charcoal,
Imperial Glass Co.
$750.00.

Candlewick
#400/74B 4-toed round bowl, ebony, 8",
Imperial Glass Co.
$325.00.

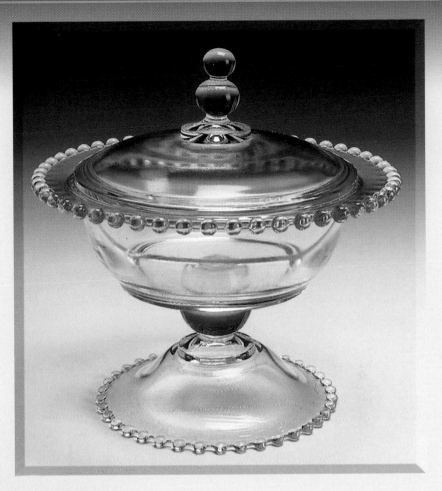

Candlewick
#400/140 beaded-foot candy and lid,
crystal, Imperial Glass Co.
$900.00.

Candlewick
#400/15 tumbler, crystal, 10 ounce,
Imperial Glass Co.
$75.00.

Candlewick
#400/18 parfait, crystal, 7 ounce,
Imperial Glass Co.
$65.00.

Candlewick
#400/187 bud vase, crystal, 7",
Imperial Glass Co.
$695.00.

Candlewick
#400/137 footed oval compote, crystal,
Imperial Glass Co.
$1,400.00.

Candlewick
#400/680 twin hurricane lamp, crystal,
Imperial Glass Co.
$1,495.00.

Candlewick
#400/194 domed foot vase, crystal,
10", Imperial Glass Co.
$650.00.

Candlewick
#400/224 candlestick, crystal, 5½",
Imperial Glass Co.
$150.00.

Candlewick
#400/195 cocktail, crystal, 4 ounce,
Imperial Glass Co.
$195.00.

Candlewick
#400/195 wine, crystal,
2 ounce, Imperial Glass Co.
$225.00.

Candlewick
#400/225 goblet, crystal,
Imperial Glass Co.
$395.00.

Candlewick
Eagle bookend, crystal,
Imperial Glass Co.
$275.00.

Candlewick
#400/242 vase with frog, crystal, 6",
Imperial Glass Co.
$495.00.

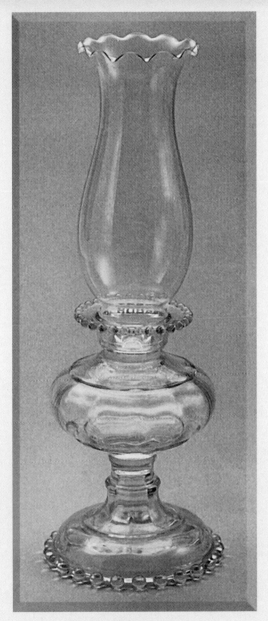

Candlewick
#400/26 hurricane lamp,
crystal, Imperial Glass Co.
$995.00.

Candlewick
#400/245 candy box, crystal, 6½",
Imperial Glass Co.
$295.00.

Candlewick
Basket, crystal,
6½",
Imperial Glass Co.
$295.00.

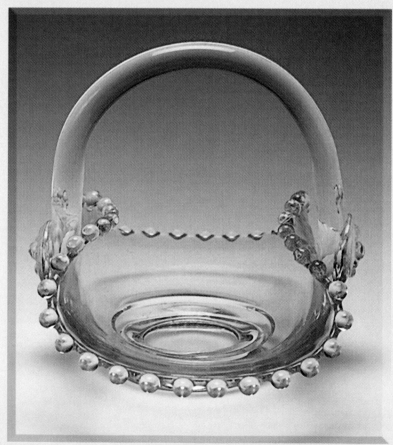

Candlewick
Banana stand with pointed edge (top), banana stand with beaded edge (bottom), crystal, Imperial Glass Co. Note the two styles of banana stands. $2,295.00.

Candlewick
#400/79 candlestick with hurricane shade, crystal with red bird and floral decoration, Imperial Glass Co. $150.00.

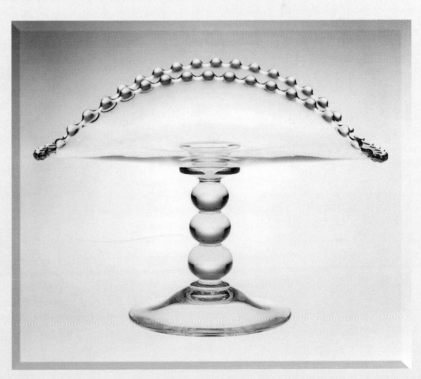

Candlewick
Bowl on stem (left) and handled
bowl (right), crystal,
Imperial Glass Co.
Bowl on stem, $350.00;
handled bowl, $150.00.

Candlewick
#400/75N lily bowl, crystal,
Imperial Glass Co.
$495.00.

Candlewick
#400/2911 condiment set, crystal decorated with orchids, Imperial Glass Co.
Bottle, $75.00 each;
tray, $35.00.

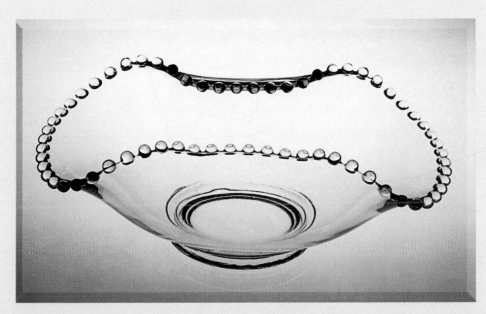

Candlewick
Whimsy bowl made from
old style basket without
a handle, crystal,
Imperial Glass Co.
$395.00.

Candlewick
Handled vase (left) and sherbet (right), crystal,
Imperial Glass Co.
Vase, $595.00; sherbet, $195.00.

Candlewick
Goblet, cut crystal,
Imperial Glass Co.
$175.00.

Candlewick
Punch bowl set, crystal
with mallard cutting,
Imperial Glass Co.
$750.00.

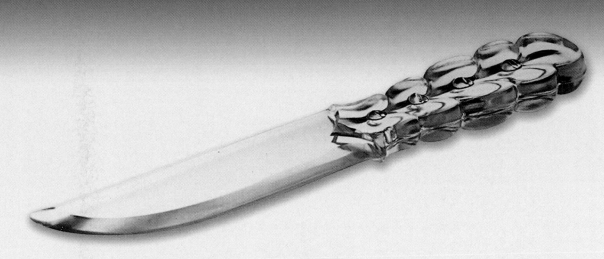

Candlewick
Knife, crystal, Imperial Glass Co.
$500.00.

Candlewick
Pitcher, crystal with amethyst foot,
Imperial Glass Co.
$1,295.00.

Candlewick
Punch bowl and cups (above) and oval snack plate with cup (below),
gold inlaid on glass, Imperial Glass Co.
Punch bowl set, $9,500.00; snack plate with cup, $350.00.

Candlewick
Handled cordial decanter,
red footed, 15 ounce,
Imperial Glass Co.
$695.00.

Candlewick
Lighting fixture, Imperial Glass Co.
$1,095.00.

Candlewick
Plate, slag, Imperial Glass Co.
$295.00.

Canterbury
Oval bowl, red, 10",
Duncan & Miller Glass Co.
$95.00.

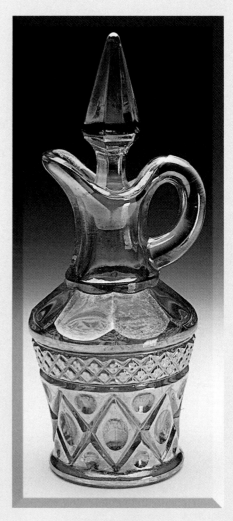

Cape Cod
#160/90 Aladdin-style candleholder, crystal, 4",
Imperial Glass Co.
$95.00.

Cape Cod
Cruet with stopper, iridescent,
Imperial Glass Co.
$75.00.

Cape Cod
Fan vase with straight top,
crystal, Imperial Glass Co.
$245.00.

Cape Cod
#160/72 birthday cake plate, crystal, 13",
Imperial Glass Co.
$425.00.

Cape Cod
Whimsy vase made from
a tumbler, crystal,
Imperial Glass Co.
$395.00.

Caprice
Cup and saucer, Mulberry,
Cambridge Glass Co.
$150.00.

Caprice
Water goblets, amber (left) and amethyst (right),
Cambridge Glass Co.
Amber, $400.00; amethyst, $350.00.

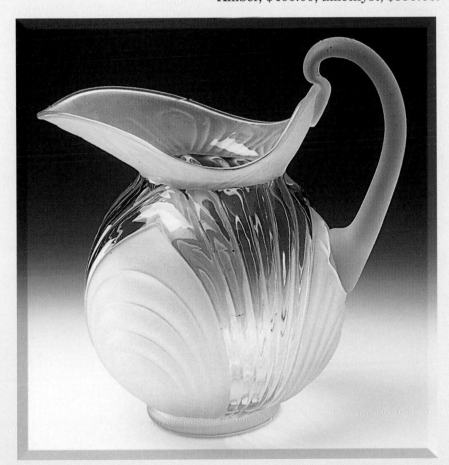

Caprice
Blue Alpine Doulton pitcher,
Cambridge Glass Co.
$5,000.00.

Caprice
Doulton-style pitcher in Farberware
holder, amethyst, 90 ounce,
Cambridge Glass Co.
$2,000.00.

Caprice
Candlestick, blue, Cambridge Glass Co.
$1,500.00.

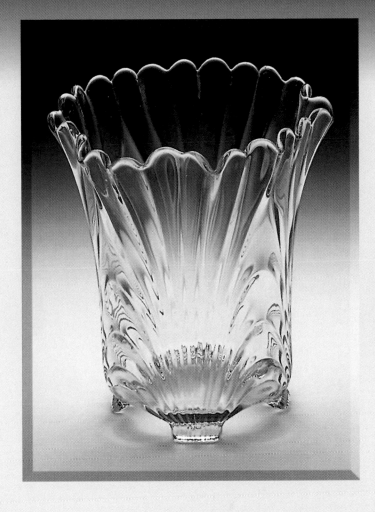

Caprice
Experimental vase, crystal, 12",
Cambridge Glass Co.
$1,500.00.

Caprice
Sherbet from unknown stemware line,
pressed crystal,
Cambridge Glass Co.
$200.00.

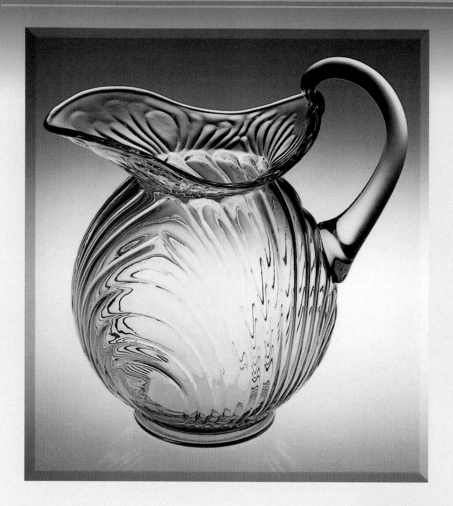

Caprice
Doulton-style pitcher,
Moonlight Blue, 90 ounce,
Cambridge Glass Co.
$4,000.00.

Caprice
Water goblet from unknown stemware
line (400?), pressed crystal,
Cambridge Glass Co.
$250.00.

Caprice
Punch bowl and candle reflectors, crystal, Cambridge Glass Co.
Punch bowl set, $2,250.00; candle reflectors, $450.00.

Caprice
Alpine comport, Moonlight Blue,
Cambridge Glass Co.
This comport is flattened half way between
the normally found one and the cheese
comport which is completely flat.
$135.00.

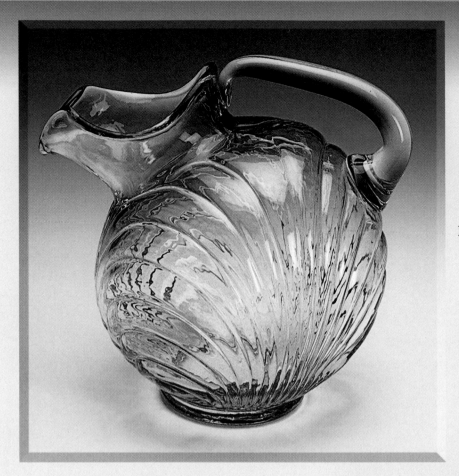

Caprice
Ball jug, Peach-Blo, 80 ounce,
Cambridge Glass Co.
$1,250.00.

Caprice
Water goblet, Topaz, 10 ounce,
Cambridge Glass Co.
$750.00.

Caprice
#726 double candlestick, Smoke,
Cambridge Glass Co.
$250.00.

Caprice
Candlestick, Carmen,
Cambridge Glass Co.
Balls must be plain to be Caprice.
$1,000.00.

Caribbean
Vase with frog, blue, 6", Duncan & Miller Glass Co.
$450.00 set.

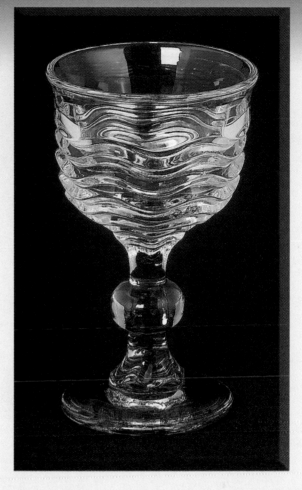

Caribbean
Cordial, blue, Duncan & Miller Glass Co.
$265.00.

Caribbean
Powder box, amber,
Duncan & Miller Glass Co.
$195.00.

Chantilly
Pristine 225 blown divided bowl, crystal, 9", Cambridge Glass Co.
$300.00.

Chantilly
Pristine 485 crescent salad plate, crystal, 9½", Cambridge Glass Co.
$175.00.

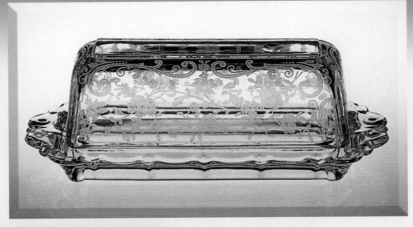

Chantilly
Quarter-pound butter dish,
crystal, Cambridge Glass Co.
$275.00.

Chantilly
#3900/575 cornucopia vase, crystal,
10", Cambridge Glass Co.
$225.00.

Chantilly
#278 vase, gold-encrusted Ebony, 11",
Cambridge Glass Co.
$800.00.

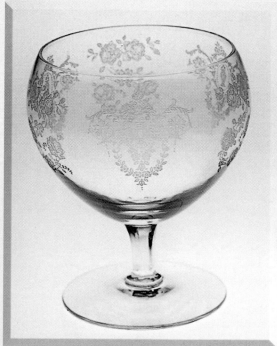

Cherokee Rose
Icer, crystal, Tiffin Glass Co.
$110.00.

Cherry Blossom
Platter, green, 9",
Jeannette Glass Co.
$1,100.00.

Cherry Blossom
Cookie jar, pink, Jeannette Glass Co.
$10,000.00.

Cherry Blossom
Grill plate, Jadite,
Jeannette Glass Co.
$125.00.

Cherry Blossom
Five-part relish tray, pink,
10½", Jeannette Glass Co.
$1,000.00.

Cherry Blossom
Plate, pink, odd size flanged
edge, Jeannette Glass Co.
$125.00.

Chintz
#2496 cream soup,
Fostoria Glass Co.
$95.00.

Chintz
#6023 footed salad bowl, 9¼", Fostoria Glass Co.
$310.00.

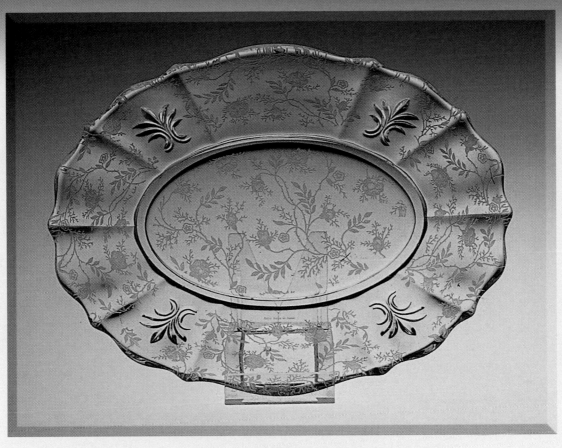

Chintz
#2496 platter, Fostoria Glass Co.
$110.00.

Chintz
Dinner bell, crystal, Fostoria Glass Co.
$125.00.

Chintz
#2586 Sani-cut syrup, crystal,
Fostoria Glass Co.
Note the two different styles.
$450.00 each.

Chintz
Cigarette box, crystal,
Fostoria Glass Co.
$150.00.

Cleo
#437 candlestick, amber, 9",
Cambridge Glass Co.
$150.00.

Cleo
#94 vase, amber, 7" x 8¼",
Cambridge Glass Co.
$150.00.

Cleo
Aero Optic vase, Emerald green, 12",
Cambridge Glass Co.
$300.00.

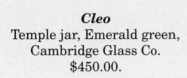

Cleo
Temple jar, Emerald green,
Cambridge Glass Co.
$450.00.

Cleo
#1070 pinch decanter, Peach-Blo, 36 ounce,
Cambridge Glass Co.
$350.00.

Cleo
#3500/13 sugar basket,
Willow blue,
Cambridge Glass Co.
$600.00.

Cleo
Sugar sifter, tall ewer, and tray, Peach-Blo, Cambridge Glass Co.
Sugar sifter, $250.00; ewer, $100.00; tray, $75.00.

Cleo
Center-handled decagon sandwich tray, Royal blue, 11", Cambridge Glass Co.
$100.00.

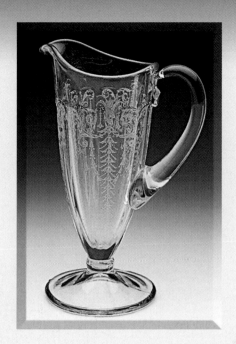

Cleo

#813 sugar sifter (left) and #816 ewer creamer (right), Willow blue, Cambridge Glass Co. Sugar sifter, $700.00; ewer creamer, $200.00.

Cleo
Pitcher, Willow blue,
Cambridge Glass Co.
$750.00.

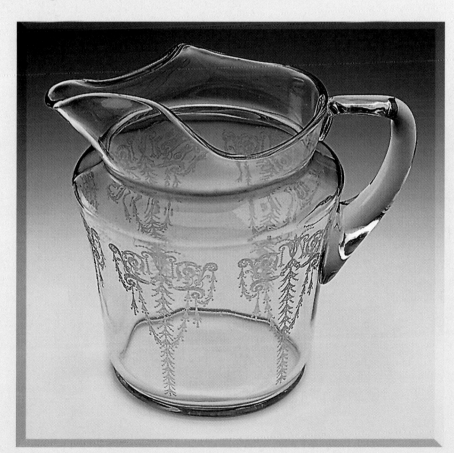

Cleo
#747 candlestick, Peach-Blo, 3",
Cambridge Glass Co.
$125.00.

Cleo
Gravy boat, Willow blue,
Cambridge Glass Co.
$495.00.

Cleo
#955 pitcher, Willow blue, 62 ounce,
Cambridge Glass Co.
$750.00.

Coca-Cola®
Ashtray, Akro Agate Co.
$300.00.

Coca-Cola®
Ashtray, Akro Agate Co.
$500.00.

Colonial
Beaded top pitcher without ice
lip, green, 7¾",
Hocking Glass Co.
$1,200.00.

Colonial
Beaded top pitcher, pink,
Hocking Glass Co.
$1,200.00.

Colonial
Sugar bowl (right) and creamer
(bottom), white, creamer is 5" and
holds 16 ounce, Hocking Glass Co.
Sugar bowl, $45.00;
creamer, $65.00.

Colonial
Footed tumbler, Royal Ruby,
10 ounce,
Hocking Glass Co.
$175.00.

Colonial
Tab-handled berry, pink,
Hocking Glass Co.
$125.00.

Colonial Block
Footed juice tumbler, green, 5¼",
5 ounce, Hazel-Atlas Glass Co.
$75.00.

Colonial Block
Creamer, Ritz blue,
Hazel-Atlas Glass Co.
$200.00.

Coronation
Tab-handled berry, green, 4¼",
Hocking Glass Co.
$95.00.

Coronation
Berry with no handles, pink, 4¼",
Hocking Glass Co.
$80.00.

Coronation
Crescent salad plate, pink, 7½",
Hocking Glass Co.
$125.00.

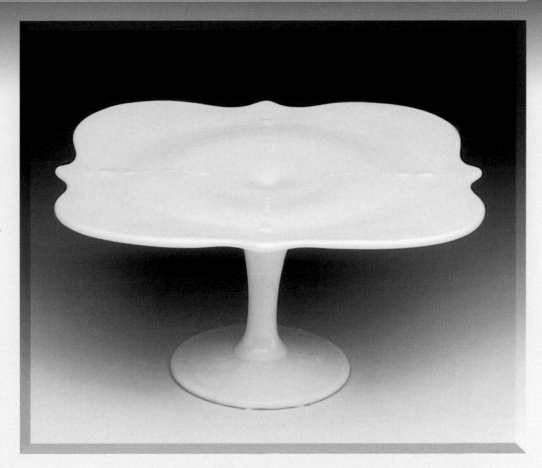

"Crow's Foot"
Cake stand, milk glass,
Paden City Glass Co.
$295.00.

"Crow's Foot"
Oval bowl, black,
Paden City Glass Co.
$125.00.

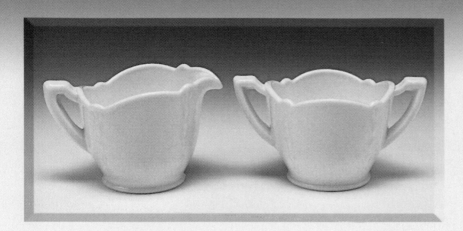

"Crow's Foot"
Creamer and sugar, opal,
Paden City Glass Co.
$75.00 each.

"Crow's Foot"
Punch bowl set, red, Paden City Glass Co.
$500.00.

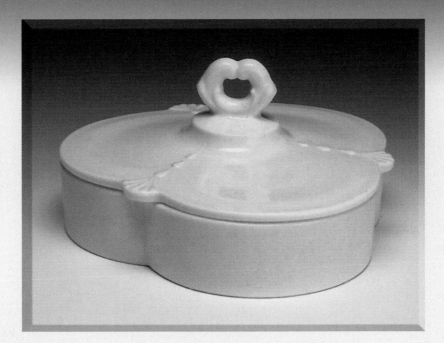

"Crow's Foot"
Three-part candy, opal,
Paden City Glass Co.
$175.00.

"Crow's Foot"
Gravy bowl and oval fluted bowl, red,
fluted bowl 10¾", Paden City Glass Co.
Gravy bowl, $140.00; fluted bowl, $95.00.

Crystolite
Gardenia bowl, Dawn, 12",
A. H. Heisey & Co.
$300.00.

Crystolite
Cocktail shaker, crystal,
A. H. Heisey & Co.
$300.00.

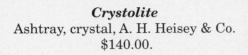

Crystolite
Ashtray, crystal, A. H. Heisey & Co.
$140.00.

Crystolite
Vase and goblet, crystal,
A. H. Heisey & Co.
Vase, $325.00; goblet, $250.00.

Crystolite
Sweet pea vase, crystal,
A. H. Heisey & Co.
$350.00.

Cube
Ruffled plate, green, 8",
Jeannette Glass Co.
$65.00.

Cube
Powder jar, blue, Jeannette Glass Co.
$295.00

Cube
Powder jar, canary yellow,
Jeannette Glass Co.
$295.00.

Cube
Footed three-part relish, pink,
Jeannette Glass Co.
$125.00.

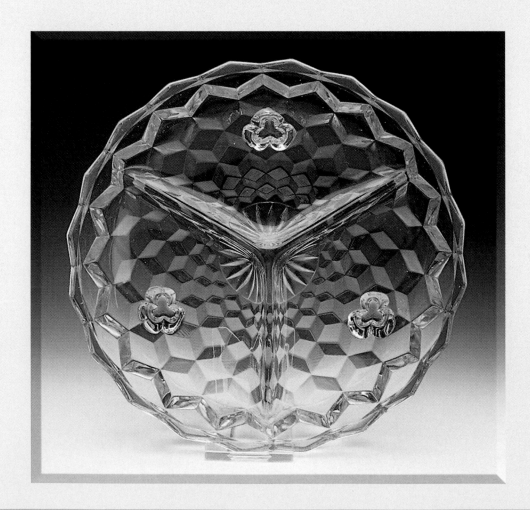

Cube
Tab-handled berry bowl, pink,
Jeannette Glass Co.
$125.00.

"Cupid"
Center-handled bowl,
gold decorated amber,
Paden City Glass Co.
$325.00.

"Cupid"
Mayonnaise, blue,
Paden City Glass Co.
$195.00.

"Cupid"
Comport, blue, 6¼",
Paden City Glass Co.
$325.00.

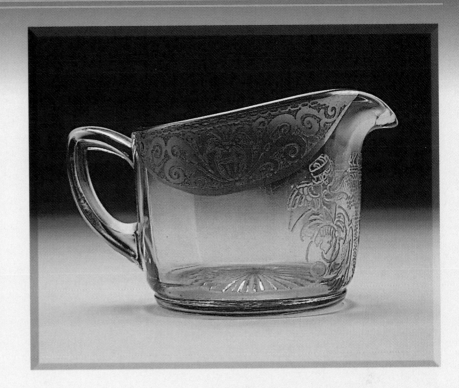

"Cupid"
Flat creamer, gold decorated pink,
Paden City Glass Co.
$175.00.

"Cupid"
Elliptical vase, gold decorated pink, 8¼",
Paden City Glass Co.
$695.00.

"Cupid"
Flat sugar, gold decorated pink,
Paden City Glass Co.
$175.00.

Dawn
#6009A cocktail shaker,
Eva Ziesel design Roundelay,
A. H. Heisey & Co.
$3,200.00.

Decagon
Canapé plate with cup, Willow blue, Cambridge Glass Co.
$100.00.

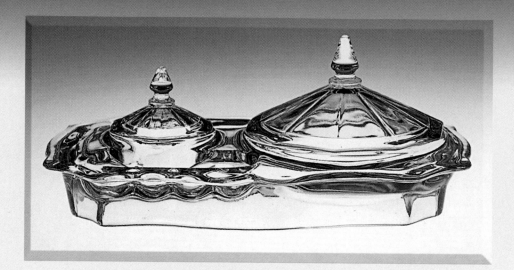

Decagon
Vanity set, Willow blue,
Cambridge Glass Co.
$350.00.

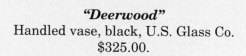

"Deerwood"
Handled vase, black, U.S. Glass Co.
$325.00.

"Deerwood"
Footed console bowl,
pink with gold trim,
10", U.S. Glass Co.
$150.00.

"Deerwood"
Cup and saucer, pink,
U.S. Glass Co.
$100.00.

Della Robia
Torte plate, pink, 14",
Westmoreland Glass Co.
$110.00.

Diamond Quilted
Candy with lid,
amber, 11½",
Imperial Glass Co.
$95.00.

Diane
#3400/4 four-footed bowl,
gold-encrusted amber, 12",
Cambridge Glass Co.
$200.00.

Diane
#1341 mushroom cordial,
amber, Cambridge Glass Co.
$65.00.

Diane
Bowl, silver decorated amethyst,
Cambridge Glass Co.
$300.00.

Diane
Decanter set, amber, Cambridge Glass Co.
Set, $900.00; tray, $150.00; pitcher, $250.00; tumbler, $80.00.

Diane
#3122 cocktail,
gold-encrusted Carmen,
Cambridge Glass Co.
$500.00.

Diane
Bowl, Crown Tuscan,
Cambridge Glass Co.
$200.00.

Diane
#3011 Statuesque ashtray (left) and cigarette box and cover (right), gold-encrusted Crown Tuscan, Cambridge Glass Co. Ashtray, $1,600.00; cigarette box and cover, $2,000.00.

Diane
#3011 Statuesque
cigarette box, crystal,
Cambridge Glass Co.
$1,200.00.

Diane
#7801 champagne with
hollow stem, crystal,
Cambridge Glass Co.
$400.00.

Diane
#498 bar glass, crystal, 2 ounce,
Cambridge Glass Co.
$95.00.

Diane
#3400/92 tumbler and
#3400/118 decanter, crystal,
tumbler is 2½ ounce;
decanter, 35 ounce,
Cambridge Glass Co.
Decanter, $275.00;
tumbler, $65.00.

Diane
#968 seafood cocktail, Emerald green (dark),
Cambridge Glass Co.
$125.00.

Diane
Cocktail churn (martini pitcher),
crystal, 60 ounce,
Cambridge Glass Co.
$1,000.00.

Diane
#1066 footed tumbler,
Emerald green (dark), 8 ounce,
Cambridge Glass Co.
$75.00.

Diane
#108 ball decanter,
Emerald green (dark), 80 ounce,
Cambridge Glass Co.
$750.00.

Diane
Cornucopia vase, crystal,
Cambridge Glass Co.
$200.00.

Diane
Cigarette box, Heatherbloom,
Cambridge Glass Co.
$500.00.

Diane
#3400 pitcher, Peach-Blo,
Cambridge Glass Co.
$600.00.

Diane
Perfume (left) and card holder (right), Heatherbloom and Crown Tuscan,
Cambridge Glass Co.
Perfume, $600.00; card holder, $500.00.

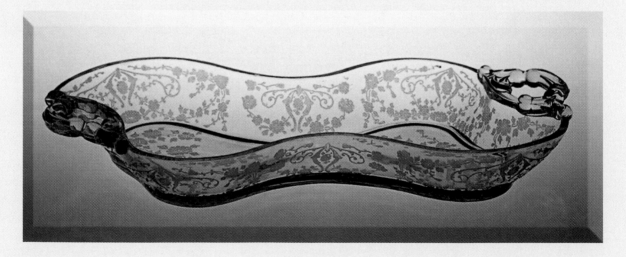

Diane
#3400 two-handled relish, Emerald green, Cambridge Glass Co.
$125.00.

Diane
#3400/92 ball decanter, Peach-Blo, Cambridge Glass Co.
$400.00.

Diane
Shaker, yellow,
Cambridge Glass Co.
$500.00.

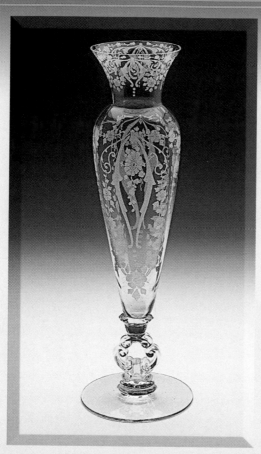

Diane
#1237 keyhole vase,
Peach-Blo, 9",
Cambridge Glass Co.
$300.00.

Dogwood
Cake plates, pink, 13" and 11", only the 11" plate is rare,
MacBeth-Evans Glass Co.
13", $165.00; 11", $1,200.00.

Dogwood
Pitcher and juice tumbler, pink,
Macbeth-Evans Glass Co.
Pitcher, $625.00;
juice tumbler, $250.00.

Dogwood
Cake plate, mother-of-pearl Cremax, Macbeth-Evans Glass Co.
$200.00.

Dogwood
Platter, pink, Macbeth-Evans Glass Co.
$750.00.

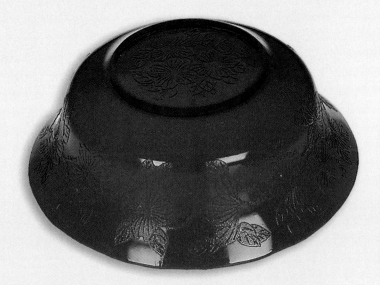

Dogwood
Berry bowl, red, Macbeth-Evans Glass Co.
$750.00.

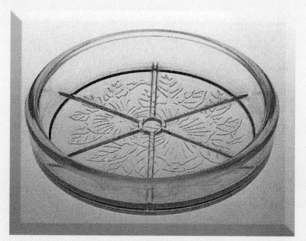

Dogwood
Coaster, pink, Macbeth-Evans Glass Co.
$695.00.

Doric
Pitcher, yellow,
Jeannette Glass Co.
$2,000.00.

Doric
Pitcher, Delphite,
Jeannette Glass Co.
$1,200.00.

Doric and Pansy
Tumbler, Ultramarine,
10 ounce, 4¼",
Jeannette Glass Co.
$595.00.

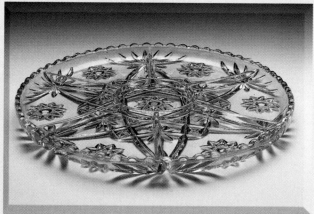

Early American Prescut, Fire King
Tray, Austalian?, Anchor Hocking Glass Co.
$200.00.

Elaine
#1402/100 Tally-Ho goblet,
frosted amber,
Cambridge Glass Co.
$250.00.

Elaine
#1402/100 Tally-Ho goblet, amber,
Cambridge Glass Co.
$85.00.

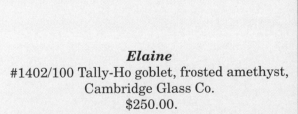

Elaine
#1402/100 Tally-Ho goblet, frosted amethyst,
Cambridge Glass Co.
$250.00.

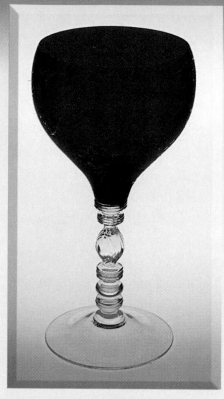

Elaine
#1402/100 Tally-Ho goblet,
frosted Carmen,
Cambridge Glass Co.
$250.00.

Elaine
#1402/100 Tally-Ho goblet,
frosted Royal blue,
Cambridge Glass Co.
$250.00.

Elaine
#1402/100 Tally-Ho goblet,
frosted Emerald green,
Cambridge Glass Co.
$250.00.

Elaine
#3500 ram's head candy, crystal, 6", Cambridge Glass Co.
$250.00.

Elaine
#485 crescent salad plate,
crystal, 4½",
Cambridge Glass Co.
$125.00.

Elaine
#3500/26 fruit basket, ram's
head bowl, Willow blue, 12",
Cambridge Glass Co.
$1,000.00.

Elaine
Top hat vase, crystal, 9",
Cambridge Glass Co.
$600.00.

Elaine
Goblet, frosted crystal, Cambridge Glass Co.
$200.00.

Elaine
#7801 champagne with hollow stem, crystal,
Cambridge Glass Co.
$300.00.

Elaine
Whimsy made from candy or urn bottom, crystal,
Cambridge Glass Co.
$200.00.

Empress
Maxfield Parrish plate, crystal,
A. H. Heisey & Co.
$650.00.

Empress
#1401 footed compotier, Moongleam, 6",
A. H. Heisey & Co.
$275.00.

Empress
Sugar, Tangerine, A. H. Heisey & Co.
$500.00.

Empress
Creamer, Tangerine, A. H. Heisey & Co.
$500.00.

Empress
Cup and saucer, Tangerine,
A. H. Heisey & Co.
$1,250.00.

English Hobnail
Water goblet, black,
Westmoreland Glass Co.
$85.00.

English Hobnail
Luncheon plate, black,
Westmoreland Glass Co.
$60.00.

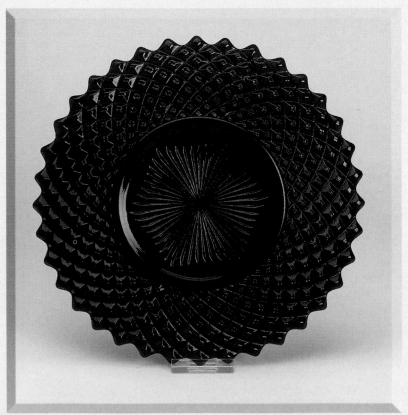

English Hobnail
Icer with patterned insert, crystal, Westmoreland Glass Co.
$65.00 set.

English Hobnail
Flat shaker, pink,
Westmoreland Glass Co.
$75.00.

Everglade
Double candleholder with epergnes, Carmen, 6", Cambridge Glass Co.
$600.00; with epergnes, $1,000.00.

Fire-King
Character mugs, Anchor Hocking Glass Co.
$30.00 each.

Fire-King
Kimberly mug, Jade-ite,
Anchor Hocking Glass Co.
$150.00.

Fire-King
Pitcher, ivory,
Anchor Hocking Glass Co.
$1,000.00.

Fire-King
Swirl pitcher, Jade-ite, 80 ounce,
Anchor Hocking Glass Co.
$1,500.00.

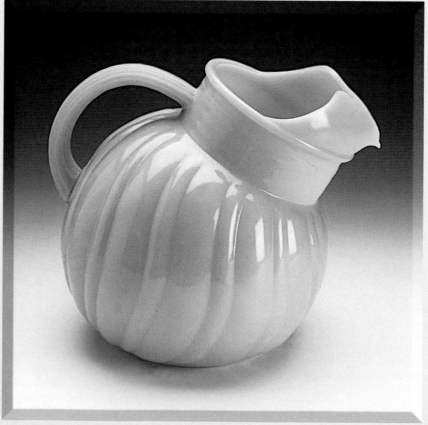

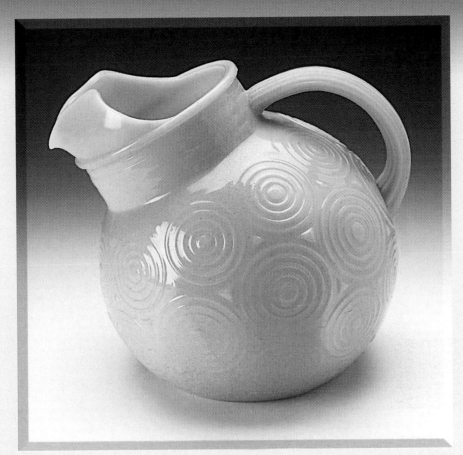

Fire-King
Target pitcher, Jade-ite, 80 ounce,
Anchor Hocking Glass Co.
$1,750.00.

Fire-King
Child's plate, Jade-ite,
Anchor Hocking Glass Co.
$550.00.

Fire-King Ovenware
Gravy or sauce boat, Jade-ite,
Anchor Hocking Glass Co.
$500.00.

Fire-King Ovenware
Casserole, Jade-ite, 2 quart,
Anchor Hocking Glass Co.
$2,000.00.

Fire-King Ovenware
Skillet, Sapphire blue,
Anchor Hocking Glass Co.
$750.00.

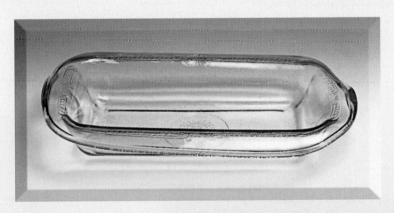

Fire-King Ovenware
Whimsey, Sapphire blue,
Anchor Hocking Glass Co.
$250.00.

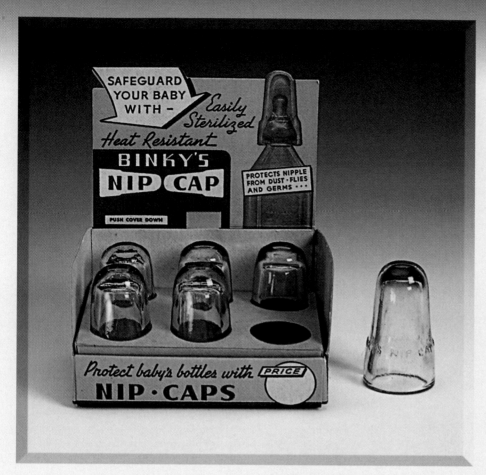

Fire-King Ovenware
Nipple covers, Sapphire blue,
Anchor Hocking Glass Co.
$1,250.00 set; $200.00 each.

Fire-King Ovenware
Dry measure, Sapphire blue,
Anchor Hocking Glass Co.
$1,000.00.

Flanders
Lamp, crystal, 12", Tiffin Glass Co.
$325.00.

Flanders
Two-handled bouillon, pink,
Tiffin Glass Co.
$135.00.

Flanders
Ashtray with cigarette rest, crystal,
2¼" x 3¾", Tiffin Glass Co.
$65.00.

Flanders
Vase, green, 6", Tiffin Glass Co.
$495.00.

Flanders
Handled parfait or Irish coffee, pink,
Tiffin Glass Co.
$195.00.

Flanders
Grapefruit or cocktail icer, pink,
Tiffin Glass Co.
$195.00.

Flanders
Nut cup, pink, Tiffin Glass Co.
$85.00.

Floragold
Square butter dish, iridescent,
5½" (right), 6¼" (bottom),
Jeannette Glass Co.
Butter dish 5½", $995.00;
butter dish 6¼", $45.00.
Note the different knob styles.

Floragold
Ruffled top (right) and plain top (bottom)
comport, iridescent, 5¼",
Jeannette Glass Co.
Ruffled top, $1,095.00;
plain top, $995.00.

Floragold
Plate on Iris blank,
Jeannette Glass Co.
$450.00.

Floral
Sugar, Cremax,
Jeannette Glass Co.
$160.00.

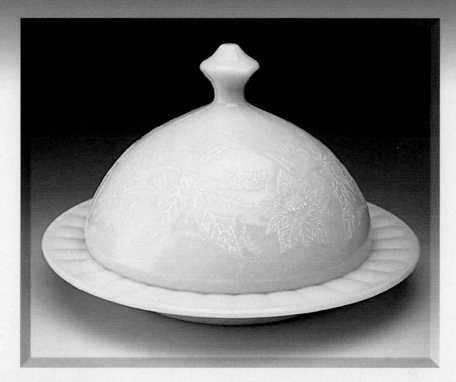

Floral
Butter dish, Cremax,
Jeannette Glass Co.
$395.00.

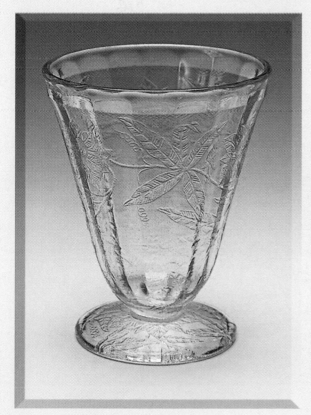

Floral
Creamer, Cremax,
Jeannette Glass Co.
$160.00.

Floral
Footed tumbler, green, 3 ounce, 3½",
Jeannette Glass Co.
$175.00.

Floral
Rose bowl with frog (left) and comport (right), green,
Jeannette Glass Co.
Rose bowl with frog insert, $525.00; frog, $725.00; comport, $995.00.

Floral
Grill plate, green,
Jeannette Glass Co.
$295.00.

Floral
Berry bowl, opaque red, 8",
Jeannette Glass Co.
$495.00.

Floral
Round bottom shaker, pink,
Jeannette Glass Co.
$300.00.

Floral
Comport (left) and cream soup (right), pink,
Jeannette Glass Co.
Comport, $950.00; cream soup, $750.00.

Floral
Ice tub, pink, Jeannette Glass Co.
$895.00.

Floral
7½" salad bowl, ruffled, pink,
Jeannette Glass Co.
$195.00.

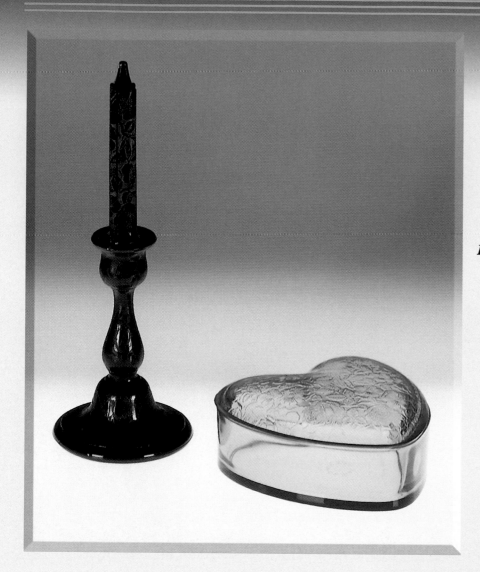

Flower Garden with Butterflies
Candle and candlestick (left),
black, and candy (right), blue,
U.S. Glass Co.
Candle, $100.00; candlestick,
$150.00; candy, $1,300.00.

Flower Garden with Butterflies
Heart-shaped candy, green,
U.S. Glass Co. $1,250.00.

Flower Garden with Butterflies
Cologne bottles with stoppers,
black (bottom right),
blue (bottom left), and crystal
with black stopper (left), 7½",
U.S. Glass Co.
Black, $400.00; blue, $350.00;
crystal with black stopper,
$250.00.

Flower Garden with Butterflies
Candy, blue with green knob, 6",
U.S. Glass Co.
$175.00.

Forest Green
Covered refrigerator jar, Forest green,
Hocking Glass Co.
$150.00.

Fuchsia
#17457 "S" stem cordial,
crystal, Tiffin Glass Co.
$125.00.

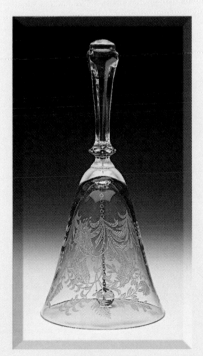

Fuchsia
Bell, crystal,
Tiffin Glass Co.
$85.00.

Fuchsia
Chinese hurricane, crystal, 12",
Tiffin Glass Co.
$300.00.

Fuchsia
Cocktail shaker, crystal,
Tiffin Glass Co.
$395.00.

Fuchsia
#9739 bitters bottle, crystal, 5 ounce,
Tiffin Glass Co.
$495.00.

Fuchsia
Cup and saucer, crystal, Tiffin Glass Co.
$95.00.

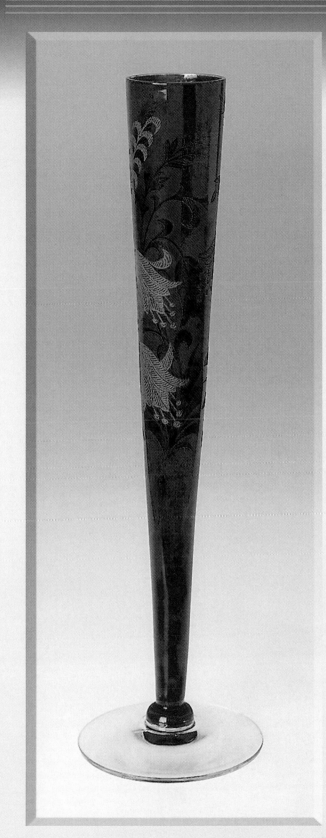

Fuchsia
#14185 bud vase, flashed red with gold,
Tiffin Glass Co.
$95.00 each.

Fuchsia
Shrimp or icer, crystal, Tiffin Glass Co.
$165.00.

Gascony
#3397 decanter, Tangerine,
A. H. Heisey & Co. $4,500.00.

Gazebo
Vases, ebony (right) and yellow (below), 10¼",
Paden City Glass Co.
Ebony, $250.00; yellow, $350.00.

Gazebo
Heart-shaped, three-part candy, blue,
Paden City Glass Co.
$250.00.

Gazebo
Five-part tray, crystal, 12",
Paden City Glass Co.
$125.00.

Georgian
Lazy Susan or cold cuts server, green, Federal Glass Co.
$900.00.

Gloria
#1070 shot glass, Carmen
with white gold, 2 ounce,
Cambridge Glass Co.
$250.00.

Georgian
Sherbet plate, Golden Glo, 6",
Federal Glass Co.
$40.00.

Gloria
Ice bucket, Willow blue,
Cambridge Glass Co.
$400.00.

Gloria
#1311 ashtray, gold-encrusted
Crown Tuscan, 4",
Cambridge Glass Co.
$850.00.

Gloria
Ivy ball, crystal,
Cambridge Glass Co.
$295.00.

Gloria
#1312 footed cigarette box, Crown
Tuscan with gold decoration,
Cambridge Glass Co.
$950.00.

Gloria
#1328 decanter and shot glass, dark Emerald green, 28 ounce, decanter, Cambridge Glass Co. Decanter, $500.00; shot glass, $75.00.

Gloria
Vase, dark Emerald green, 12",
Cambridge Glass Co.
$450.00.

Gloria
#3400 pitcher, dark Emerald green,
Cambridge Glass Co.
$750.00.

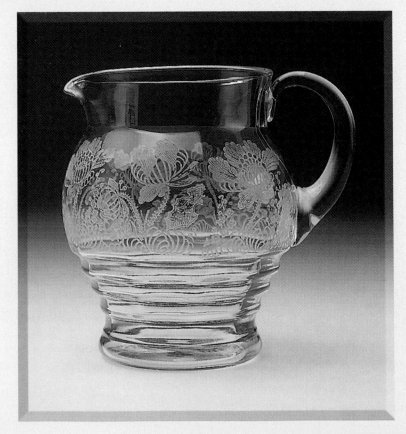

Gloria
Pitcher, Emerald green,
Cambridge Glass Co.
$250.00.

Gloria
#3400/4 four-toed bowl, Ebony with silver decoration, 12",
Cambridge Glass Co.
$400.00.

Gloria
Vase, Emerald green,
Cambridge Glass Co.
$300.00.

Gloria
#3400/92 32 ounce ball shape decanter, #8161 2 ounce tumbler,
Gold Krystol, 12", Cambridge Glass Co.
Decanter, $250.00; tumbler, $65.00.

Gloria
#646 candleholder, Ebony
with silver decoration, 5",
Cambridge Glass Co.
$100.00.

Gloria
#707 cake stand, Gold Krystol, 11", Cambridge Glass Co.
$300.00.

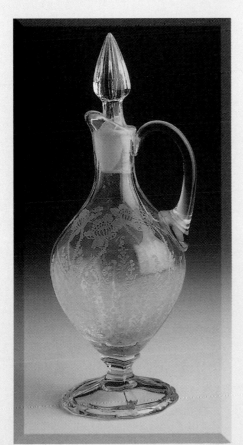

Gloria
#3400/161 oil bottle,
Gold Krystol, 6 ounce,
Cambridge Glass Co.
$450.00.

Gloria
#3011 Statuesque comport, Gold
Krystol, 9", Cambridge Glass Co.
$1,500.00.

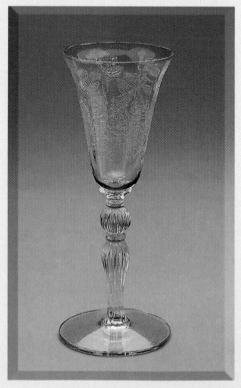

Gloria
#3035 cordial, Heatherbloom,
1 ounce,
Cambridge Glass Co.
$450.00.

Gloria
#3130 cordial, Peach-Blo, 4⅜",
Cambridge Glass Co.
$275.00.

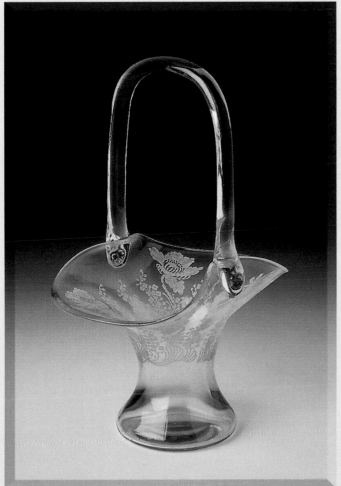

Gloria
#119 basket, Peach-Blo, 7",
Cambridge Glass Co.
$1,500.00.

Gloria
#3400 vase,
gold-encrusted Royal blue, 12",
Cambridge Glass Co.
$1,250.00.

Gloria
#3130 comport, Willow blue, 9",
Cambridge Glass Co.
$225.00.

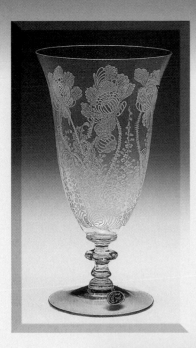

Gloria
Tumbler, Willow blue,
Cambridge Glass Co.
$95.00.

Gloria
Footed goblet,
Gold Krystol with amber stem,
Cambridge Glass Co.
$125.00.

Gloria
Decanter, Gold Krystol,
Cambridge Glass Co.
$600.00.

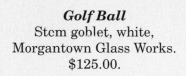

Golf Ball
Stem goblet, white,
Morgantown Glass Works.
$125.00.

Greek Key
Toothpick, crystal,
A. H. Heisey & Co.
$350.00.

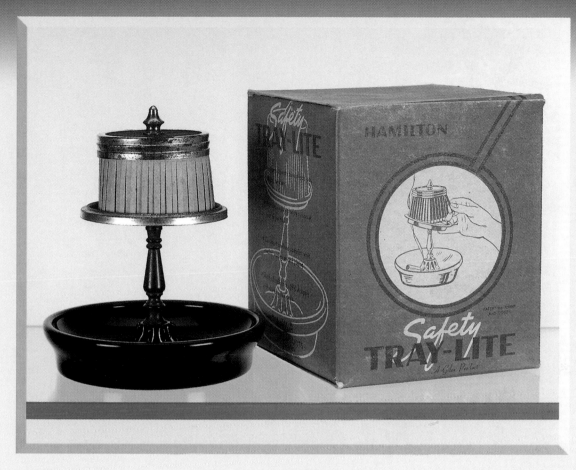

Hamilton
Safety Tray-Lite, Akro Agate Co.
$75.00.

Hermitage
#2449 three-pint pitcher,
Wisteria, Fostoria Glass Co.
$495.00.

Hex Optic
Flat pitcher, pink, 9",
96 ounce,
Jeannette Glass Co.
$150.00.

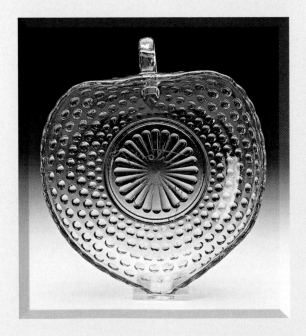

Hobnail
Heart bonbon, Lilac,
Hocking Glass Co.
$85.00.

Imperial Hunt Scene
#3075, 2802 decanter (left) and
footed fish bowl (right),
decanter is gold-encrusted amber;
footed fish bowl is green,
Cambridge Glass Co.
Decanter, $600.00;
footed fish bowl, $1,000.00.

Imperial Hunt Scene
#525 cocktail shaker, gold-encrusted amber,
Cambridge Glass Co.
$400.00.

Imperial Hunt Scene
#3077 stems, special order, gold-encrusted amber,
Cambridge Glass Co.
$90.00 – 110.00 each.

Imperial Hunt Scene
Cigar humidor, Ebony with gold,
Cambridge Glass Co.
$350.00; with domed lid $750.00.

Imperial Hunt Scene
Luncheon plate, gold with green
background, Cambridge Glass Co.
$400.00.

Imperial Hunt Scene
Shot glass, Peach-Blo,
Cambridge Glass Co.
$95.00.

Imperial Hunt Scene
Salt shaker, Peach-Blo,
Cambridge Glass Co.
$150.00.

Imperial Hunt Scene
Cup and saucer, Peach-Blo,
Cambridge Glass Co.
$85.00.

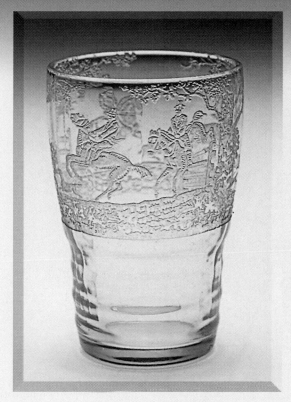

Imperial Hunt Scene
Shot glass, Emerald green,
Cambridge Glass Co.
$125.00.

Imperial Hunt Scene
Goblet, gold-encrusted Avocado,
Cambridge Glass Co.
$1,000.00.

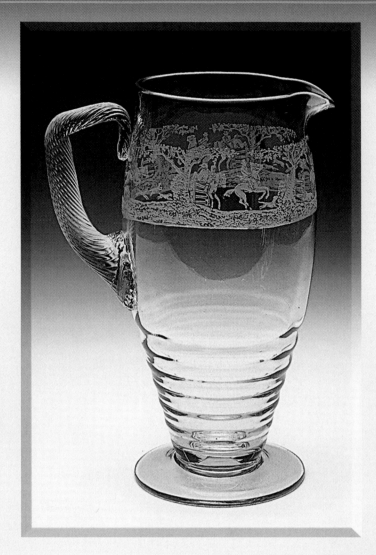

Imperial Hunt Scene
Footed pitcher, Peach-Blo with Emerald foot,
Cambridge Glass Co.
$650.00.

Imperial Hunt Scene
Sugar with lid, Peach-Blo, Cambridge Glass Co.
$150.00.

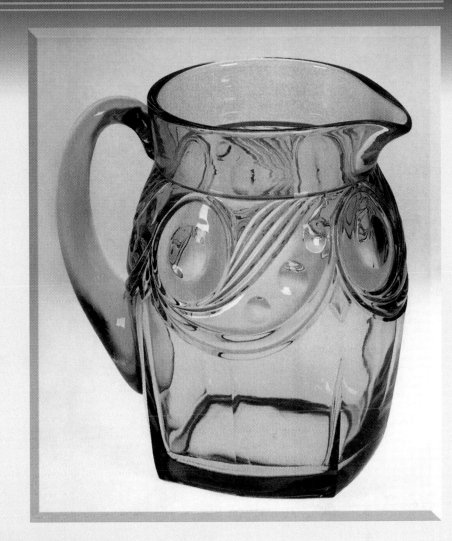

Ipswich
Pitcher, Moongleam,
A. H. Heisey & Co.
$1,000.00.

Ipswich
Candlestick with footed vase
and "A" prism, Moongleam,
A. H. Heisey & Co.
$450.00.

Iris
Corsage decorations, crystal, Jeannette Glass Co.
Footed tea, $45.00; water goblet, $40.00; wine $35.00.

Iris
Round dinner plate, crystal,
Jeannette Glass Co.
$150.00.

Iris
Odd sugar lid and regular sugar bowl, crystal,
Jeannette Glass Co.
Lid, $250.00; bowl, $11.00.

Iris
Creamer, green,
Jeannette Glass Co.
$250.00.

Iris
Demitasse cups and saucers, flashed red, flashed blue, iridescent, and flashed amethyst,
Jeannette Glass Co.
$400.00 each set.

Iris
Goblet, iridescent, 5½", 4 ounce,
Jeannette Glass Co.
$500.00.

Iris
Plastic plate, iridescent,
Jeannette Glass Co.
$50.00.

Iris
Powder jar, crystal, 5¼" diameter, 4⅝" tall with lid, Jeannette Glass Co. Knob has six flat sides.
$1,250.00.

Jamestown
Cake salver, green,
7" high, 10" diameter,
Fostoria Glass Co.
$250.00.

Jamestown
Water goblet, cobalt,
Fostoria Glass Co.
$450.00.

"Jane Ray," Fire-King
Flat soup, green, 9",
Anchor Hocking Glass Co.
$295.00.

Janice
Basket, blue, 12",
New Martinsville Glass Co.
$215.00.

Janice
Footed ice tub, Emerald green, 6",
New Martinsville Glass Co./ Viking
$250.00.

Janice
Basket/footed ice tub, blue, 6",
New Martinsville Glass Co.
$1,500.00.

Janice
Footed ice tub, blue, 6",
New Martinsville Glass Co.
$250.00.

Jubilee
Cordial, yellow, 4", 1 ounce,
Lancaster Glass Co.
$395.00.

Jubilee
Cocktail, yellow, 4⅞", 3 ounce,
Lancaster Glass Co.
$150.00.

Jubilee
Oyster cocktail, yellow, 4¾",
4 ounce,
Lancaster Glass Co.
$75.00.

Jubilee
Sherbet, yellow, 3",
8 ounce,
Lancaster Glass Co.
$70.00.

Jubilee
Three-footed bowl, yellow, 13", Lancaster Glass Co.
$225.00.

Jubilee
Bud vase, pink,
Lancaster Glass Co.
$125.00.

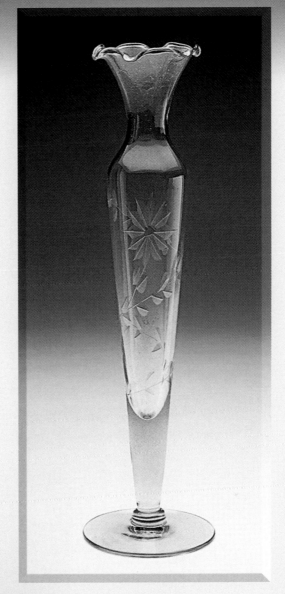

Jubilee
Candlestick, crystal,
Lancaster Glass Co.
$65.00.

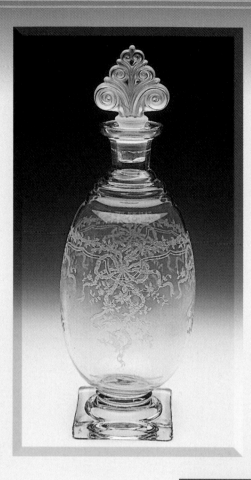

June
#4020 footed decanter, yellow,
Fostoria Glass Co.
$3,000.00.

June
Footed oil bottle, pink,
Fostoria Glass Co.
$995.00.

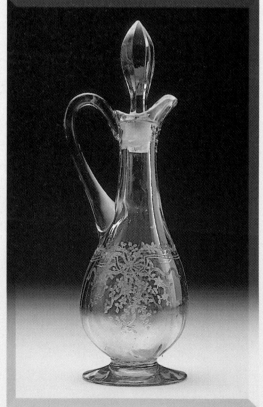

June Night
Pitcher, crystal, Tiffin Glass Co.
$595.00.

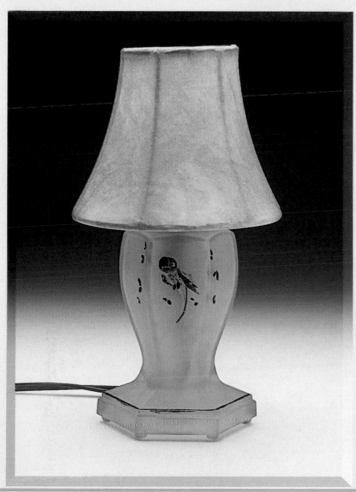

Jungle Assortment
Parrot lamp, Tiffin Glass Co.
$100.00.

King's Crown
Punch set, crystal with red
trim, U.S. Glass Co.
$1,150.00.

King's Crown
Party server, crystal with red trim,
24", U.S. Glass Co.
$350.00.

King's Crown
15-piece punch set, crystal with red trim,
U.S. Glass Co.
$1,250.00.

Kitchenware
Canister, blue, 40 ounce,
Hocking Glass Co.
$300.00.

Kitchenware
Rolling pin, Chalaine blue,
McKee Glass Co.
$2,500.00.

Kitchenware
Batter bowl, blue,
Hocking Glass Co.
$295.00.

Kitchenware, Saunders
Reamer, black,
McKee Glass Co.
$1,500.00.

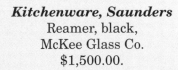

Laced Edge "Katy Blue"
Basket bowl, blue,
Imperial Glass Co.
$295.00.

Laced Edge
Spittoon vase, green, Imperial Glass Co.
$300.00.

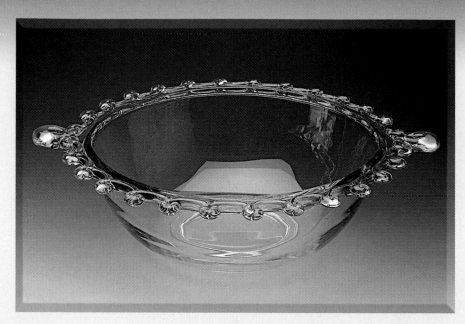

Lariat
Handled bowl, crystal, 12",
A. H. Heisey & Co.
$250.00.

Lariat
Blackout lights and plate, lights are crystal; plate is black, A. H. Heisey & Co.
Plate, $850.00; blackout lights, $300.00 pair.

Lariat
Horse head candy, crystal,
A. H. Heisey & Co.
$1,400.00.

Lariat
Goblet, crystal,
A. H. Heisey & Co.
$450.00.

Lariat
Two-handled trophy vase, crystal,
A. H. Heisey & Co.
$625.00.

Laurel
Champagne/high sherbet,
French Ivory, 5",
McKee Glass Co.
$75.00.

Laurel
Flat soup, Poudre Blue, 7⅛",
McKee Glass Co.
$90.00.

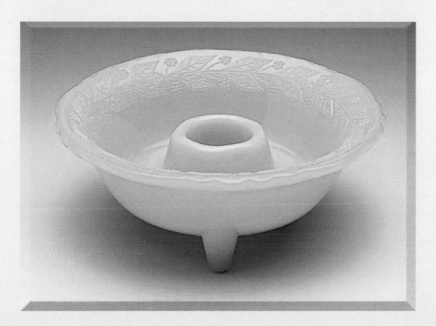

Laurel
Three-footed candlestick, green,
McKee Glass Co.
$150.00.

Lincoln Inn
Pitcher and tumbler, blue,
Fenton Glass Co.
Pitcher, $800.00; tumbler, $35.00.

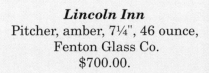

Lincoln Inn
Pitcher, amber, 7¼", 46 ounce,
Fenton Glass Co.
$700.00.

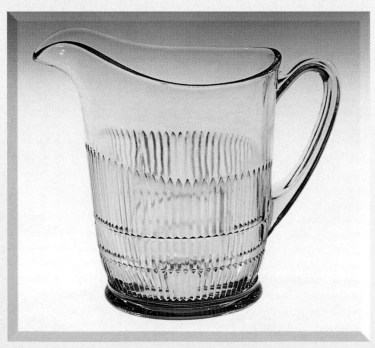

Lincoln Inn
Center-handled server, cobalt blue,
Fenton Glass Co.
$175.00.

Lincoln Inn
Center-handled sandwich
server, red,
Fenton Glass Co.
$175.00.

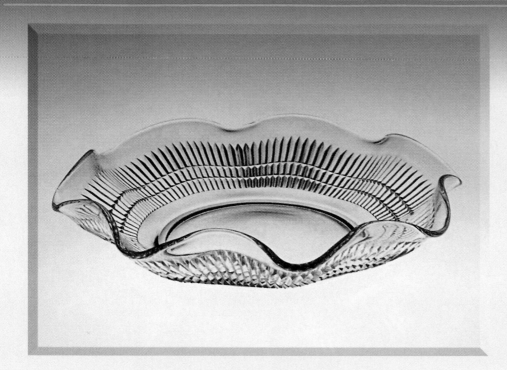

Lincoln Inn
Ruffled bowl, pink, 11",
Fenton Glass Co.
$100.00.

Lodestar
Double candlestick (left) and single candleblock (right), Dawn, A. H. Heisey & Co.
Double candlestick, $350.00; single candleblock, $250.00.

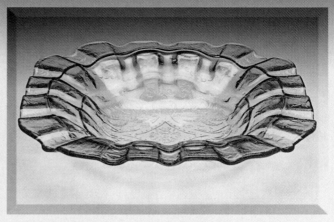

Madrid
Whimsey ruffled cigar ashtray, Golden Glo,
Federal Glass Co.
$350.00.

Madrid
Lazy Susan, Golden Glo, Federal Glass Co.
$995.00.

Manhattan
Juice pitcher, Royal Ruby,
Anchor Hocking Glass Co.
$795.00.

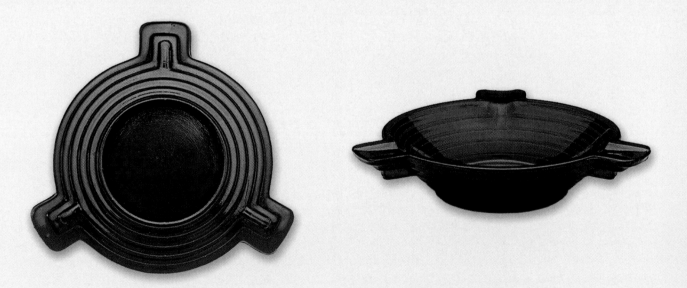

Manhattan
Ashtray, Royal Ruby, 4", Anchor Hocking Glass Co.
$50.00.

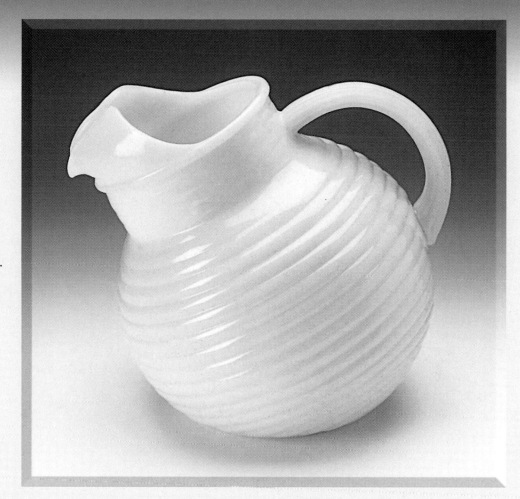

Manhattan
Pitcher, ivory, 80 ounce,
Anchor Hocking Glass Co.
$1,000.00.

Manhattan
Cereal bowl, pink, Anchor Hocking Glass Co.
$200.00.

Marjorie
Oil bottle, green,
Cambridge Glass Co.
$495.00.

Mayfair
Cream soup, crystal,
Hocking Glass Co.
$85.00.

Mayfair
Round cups, pink, thick or thin, Hocking Glass Co.
$350.00 each.

Mayfair
Footed, flared vase, crystal,
Hocking Glass Co.
$2,000.00.

Mayfair
Console bowls, green (top), pink (middle), and frosted pink (bottom), Hocking Glass Co.
Green, $5,750.00; pink, $5,750.00; frosted pink, $2,750.00.

Mayfair
Miniature berry bowl, pink, 3¾" square x 1⅝" deep,
Hocking Glass Co.
$995.00.

Mayfair
Cordial, green, 3¾", 1 ounce,
Hocking Glass Co.
$995.00.

Mayfair
Five-part relish, pink, Hocking Glass Co.
$1,250.00.

Mayfair
Footed shaker, pink,
Hocking Glass Co.
$5,000.00.

Mayfair
Claret, pink, 5¼", 4½ ounce,
Hocking Glass Co.
$1,000.00.

Mayfair
Vase, pink,
Hocking Glass Co.
$5,995.00.

Mayfair
Covered bowl, yellow, 10", Hocking Glass Co.
$995.00.

Mayfair
Butter dish (left) and sugar with lid (right), yellow,
Hocking Glass Co.
Butter dish, $1,300.00; sugar with lid, $1,350.00.

Mayfair
Cookie jar, yellow,
Hocking Glass Co.
$895.00.

Mayfair
Off-center sherbet plate, yellow,
Hocking Glass Co.
$135.00.

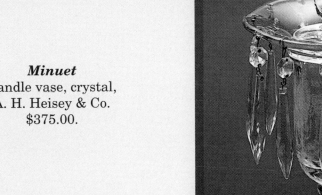

Minuet
Candle vase, crystal,
A. H. Heisey & Co.
$375.00.

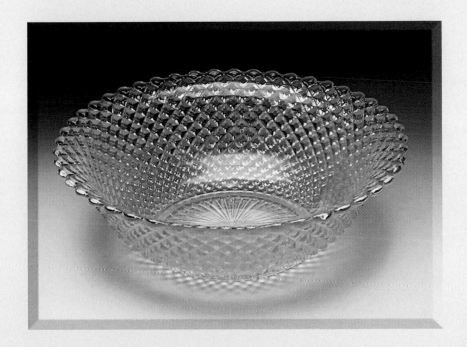

Miss America
Bowl, irridescent,
Hocking Glass Co.
$125.00.

Miss America
Juice tumbler, blue,
Hocking Glass Co.
$150.00.

Miss America
Dinner plate, blue,
Hocking Glass Co.
$150.00.

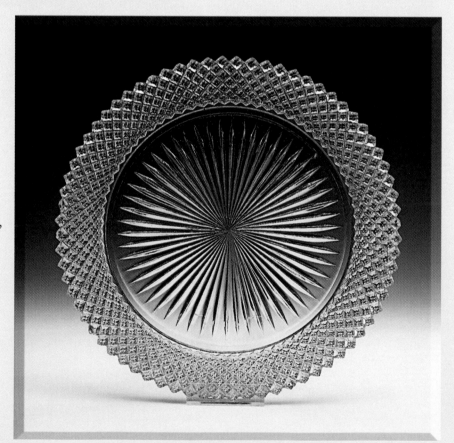

Miss America
Water tumbler, Jade-ite,
Hocking Glass Co.
$150.00.

Miss America
Salad plate, Jade-ite,
Hocking Glass Co.
$150.00.

Miss America
Five-part relish or Lazy Susan, pink, Hocking Glass Co.
$6,250.00.

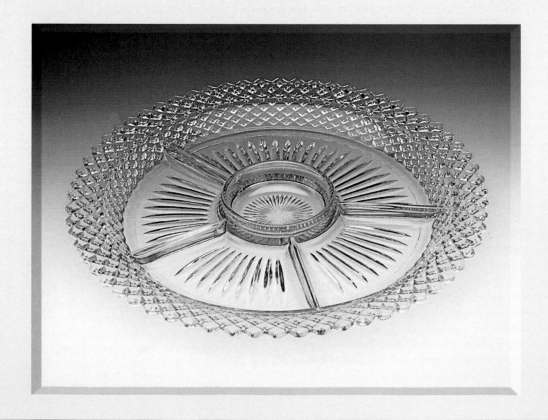

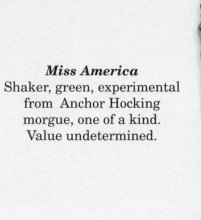

Miss America
Shaker, green, experimental
from Anchor Hocking
morgue, one of a kind.
Value undetermined.

Miss America
Bowl, Royal Ruby, 11", shallow,
Hocking Glass Co.
$900.00.

Miss America
A selection of pieces in Royal Ruby, Hocking Glass Co.
Plate, 8½", $165.00; footed juice tumbler, 4¾", 5 ounce, $300.00; wine goblet, 3 ounce, $325.00;
juice tumbler, 4", 5 ounce, $275.00; cup, $300.00; saucer, $75.00; curved-in bowl, 8", $600.00;
sherbet, 3⁵⁄₁₆", $150.00; creamer, $235.00; two-handled sugar, $235.00;
water goblet, 5⁷⁄₁₆", 8¾ ounce, $325.00.

Moderntone
Cup and saucer, pink,
Hazel-Atlas Glass Co.
$75.00.

Moderntone
16-piece child's set in box,
white, Hazel-Atlas Glass Co.
$450.00.

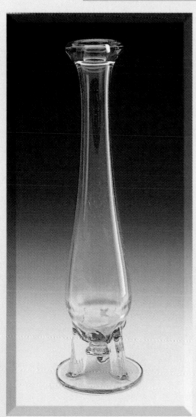

Moondrops
"Rocket" bud vase, pink, 8½",
New Martinsville Glass Co.
$275.00.

Moondrops
Powder jar, pink, New
Martinsville Glass Co.
$225.00.

Moondrops
Tumbler, black,
New Martinsville Glass Co.
$75.00.

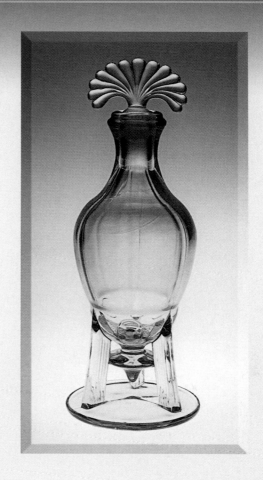

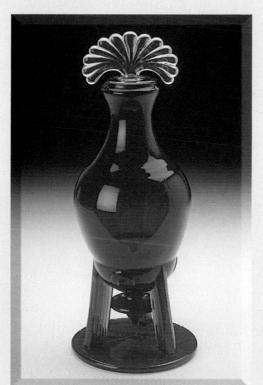

Moondrops
"Rocket" decanters, crystal, Emerald green, and pink;
New Martinsville Glass Co.
Crystal, $450.00; Emerald green, $495.00;
pink, $495.00.

Moondrops
"Rocket" decanters and wine, red and Ritz blue, New Martinsville Glass Co.
Decanters, $550.00 each; wine $65.00.

Moondrops
Cream soup, ruby,
New Martinsville Glass Co.
$100.00.

Moondrops
Covered casserole, Ritz blue, 9¾",
New Martinsville Glass Co.
$250.00.

Moondrops
Candlesticks, red, 6",
New Martinsville Glass Co.
$150.00 pair.

Moonstone
Sherbet, opalescent green,
Anchor Hocking Glass Co.
$65.00.

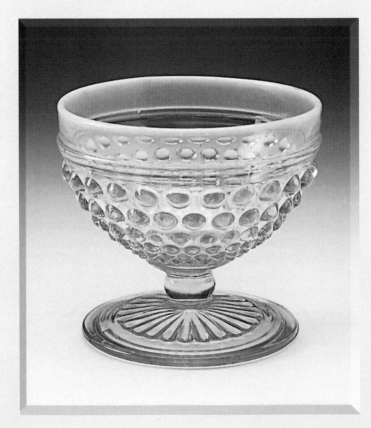

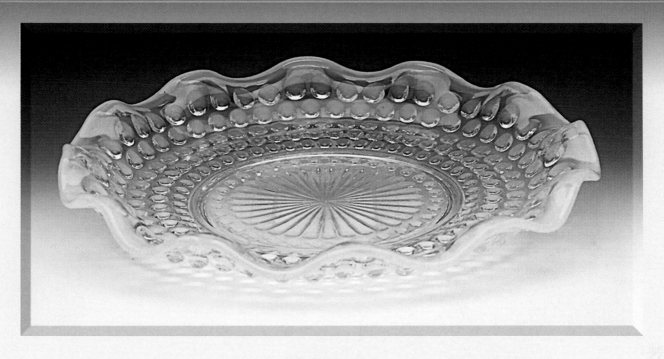

Moonstone
Ruffled plate, opalescent, 11⅛", Anchor Hocking Glass Co.
$150.00.

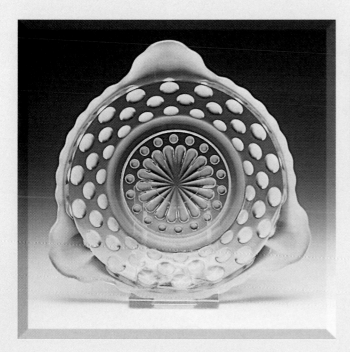

Moonstone
Ashtray, opalescent, 4", Anchor Hocking Glass Co.
$95.00.

Moonstone
Dinner plate, opalescent,
Anchor Hocking Glass Co.
$125.00.

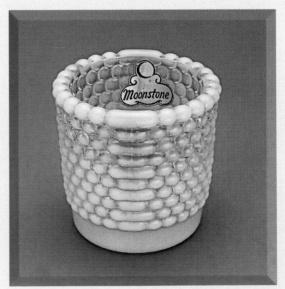

Moonstone
Tumbler (left) and toothpick holder (right),
both are opalescent, tumbler is 5", 10 ounce,
Anchor Hocking Glass Co.
Tumbler, $100.00; toothpick, $85.00.

Moonstone
Divided relish, opalescent,
Anchor Hocking Glass Co.
$95.00.

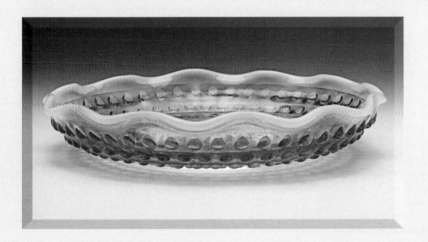

Moonstone
Ruffled bowl, red-flashed, 7¾",
Anchor Hocking Glass Co.
$100.00.

Moonstone
Divided, crimped bowl, pink opalescent,
7½", Anchor Hocking Glass Co.
$110.00.

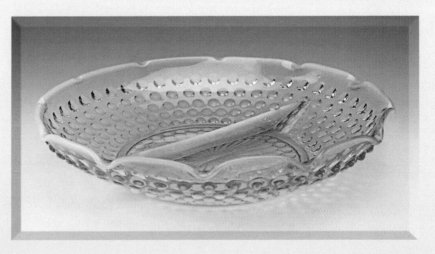

Moonstone
Bowl, red flashed, 7¾",
Anchor Hocking Glass Co.
$65.00.

Moonstone
Two-handled ruffled bowl,
red flashed,
Anchor Hocking Glass Co.
$85.00.

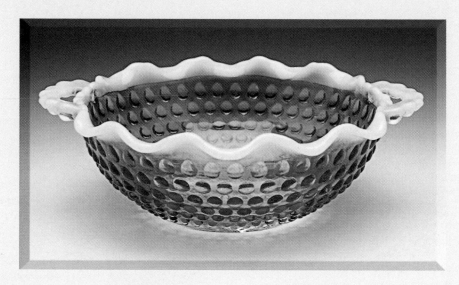

Moonstone
Cup and saucer, yellow opalescent,
Anchor Hocking Glass Co.
$125.00.

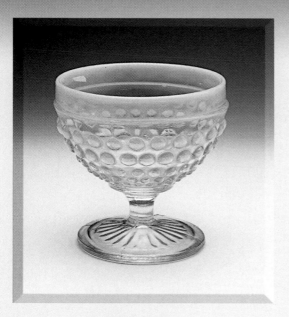

Moonstone
Sherbet, yellow opalescent,
Anchor Hocking Glass Co.
$65.00.

Morgan
Decanter and whiskey, pink,
Central Glass Co.
Decanter, $495.00; whiskey, $100.00.

Morgan
Vase with ruffled top in holder,
green, 10", Central Glass Co.
$595.00.

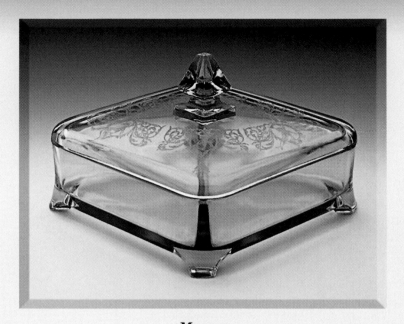

Morgan
Diamond-shaped, divided, footed candy dish, pink,
Central Glass Co.
$495.00.

Morgan
Bud vase, black with gold
decoration, 10",
Central Glass Co.
$395.00.

Morgan
Ice tub, pink, Central Glass Co.
$650.00.

Mt. Vernon
Candelabrum, Carmen #38, 13½",
Cambridge Glass Co.
$1,500.00.

Mt. Vernon
Two-handled comport, Emerald green
(dark) #77, 5½", Cambridge Glass Co.
$125.00.

Nautical
Comport, opalescent blue,
Duncan & Miller Glass Co.
$750.00.

Navarre
Carafe, crystal, 16 ounce,
Fostoria Glass Co.
$1,000.00.

Navarre
#2083 salad dressing bottle, crystal,
Fostoria Glass Co.
$495.00.

Navarre
Carafe, crystal, 32 ounce,
Fostoria Glass Co.
$1,200.00.

Navarre
Bell (left), crystal,
Fostoria Glass Co.
$75.00.

Navarre
Dinner bell (right), green,
Fostoria Glass Co.
$150.00.

No. 610 "Pyramid"
Ice bucket and lid, yellow, Indiana Glass Co.
$895.00.

No. 620 "Daisy"
Plate, blue, Indiana Glass Co.
$100.00.

No. 612 "Horseshoe"
Grill plates, yellow (left), and green (right), 10⅜",
Indiana Glass Co.
Yellow, $150.00; green, $125.00.

No. 622 "Pretzel"
Cup, Terrace Green,
Indiana Glass Co.
$125.00.

No. 624 "Christmas Candy"
Bowl, Terrace Green, 9½",
Indiana Glass Co.
$625.00.

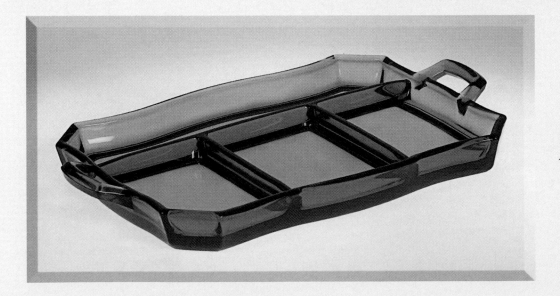

Octagon
Relish tray, Dawn
A.H. Heisey & Co.
$325.00.

Octagon, Ribbed
#1231 rum pot, cobalt,
A.H. Heisey & Co.
$2,600.00.

Old Colony
Comport, 9", Hocking Glass Co.
$995.00.

Old Colony
Water, 4½" 9 ounce, flat juice,
3½", 5 ounce,
Hocking Glass Co.
Water, $22.00; flat juice, $150.00.

Old Colony
Vase, pink, 7", Hocking Glass Co.
$750.00.

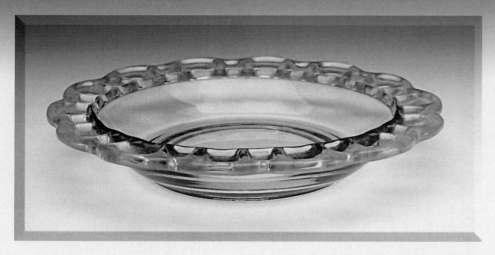

Old Colony
Bowl, pink opalescent, 7¾",
Hocking Glass Co.
$195.00.

Old English
Pitcher, pink, Indiana Glass Co.
$350.00.

Old Sandwich
Cup and saucer, Moongleam,
A. H. Heisey & Co.
$175.00.

Old English
Footed tumblers, pink, 5½" and 4½",
Indiana Glass Co.
5½", $45.00; 4½", $35.00.

Old Sandwich
Basket, A. H. Heisey & Co.
$800.00.

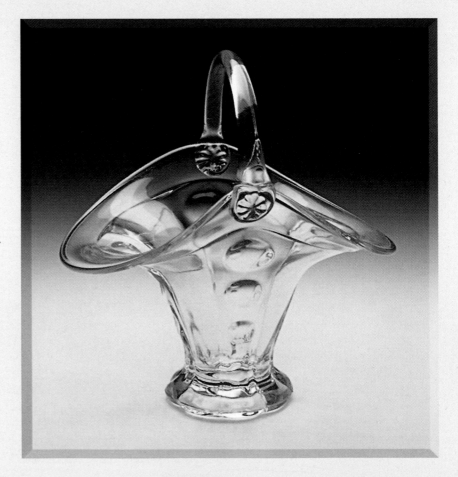

Old Williamsburg
Two-light candelabrum, cobalt, A. H. Heisey & Co.
$1,750.00.

Orchid
#5012 square footed bud
vase, crystal, 12",
A. H. Heisey & Co.
$225.00.

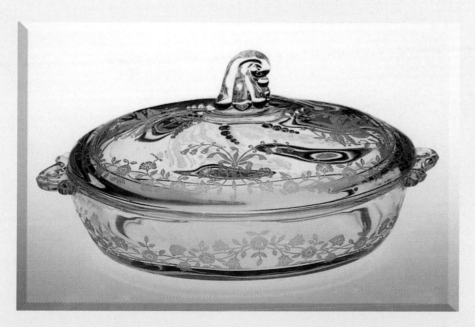

Orchid
Waverly lemon dish, crystal,
A. H. Heisey & Co.
$750.00.

Orchid
Finger bowl, crystal,
A. H. Heisey & Co.
$160.00.

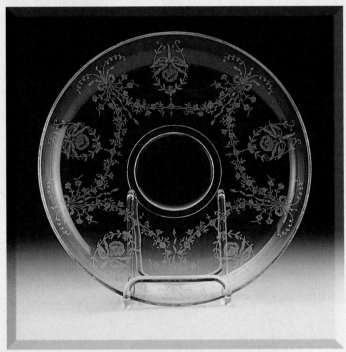

Orchid
Bowl, crystal, 14",
A. H. Heisey & Co.
$350.00.

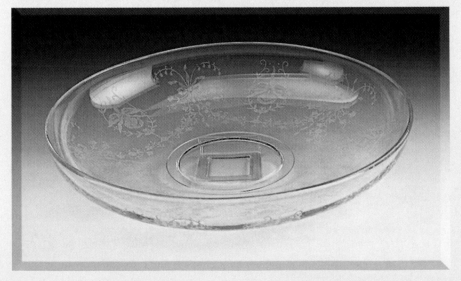

Orchid
#4205 bud vase, crystal, 8",
A. H. Heisey & Co.
$400.00.

Orchid
Vase, crystal, 14",
A. H. Heisey & Co.
$700.00.

"Orchid"
Vase, black, 8",
Paden City Glass Co.
$295.00.

"Orchid"
Vase, green, 10",
Paden City Glass Co.
$195.00.

"Orchid"
Vase, red, 10",
Paden City Glass Co.
$325.00.

"Orchid"
Vase, red, 10",
Paden City Glass Co.
$400.00.

"Orchid"
Comport on Crow's Foot,
red, 6⅝",
Paden City Glass Co.
$165.00.

"Orchid"
Cupped vase, red, 6½",
Paden City Glass Co.
$225.00.

Ovide
Sugar bowl (left) and creamer (right), Art Deco decorated, Hazel-Atlas Glass Co.
$110.00 each.

Oyster & Pearl
Ruffled edge bowl, crystal,
Anchor Hocking Glass Co.
$45.00.

Paneled Grape
Three-piece epergne set, milk glass,
Westmoreland Glass Co.
$495.00.

Paneled Grape
Three-lite candelabra, milk glass, Westmoreland Glass Co.
$165.00.

Paneled Grape
Wall pocket, milk glass,
Westmoreland Glass Co.
$150.00.

Paneled Grape
Herb planter, milk glass, 12" x 6½",
Westmoreland Glass Co.
$110.00.

"Parrot"
Footed tumbler (Madrid mould),
amber, 5½", 10 ounce,
Federal Glass Co.
$175.00.

"Parrot"
Pitcher, green, 8½",
80 ounce,
Federal Glass Co.
$3,195.00.

"Parrot"
Butter dish, Golden Glo,
Federal Glass Co.
$1,350.00.

"Parrot"
Sherbet, green, 4¼",
Federal Glass Co.
$1,450.00.

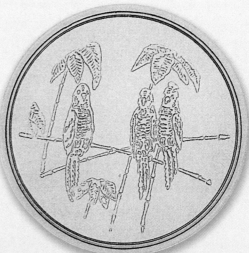

"Parrot"
Round hot plate (right), Springtime green, 5",
Federal Glass Co.
$995.00.

"Parrot"
Paperweight (left), Golden Glo,
Federal Glass Co.
$300.00.

Patrician
Sugar with rare lid, amber,
Federal Glass Co.
$250.00.

Patrician
Vase, green, Federal Glass Co.
$995.00.

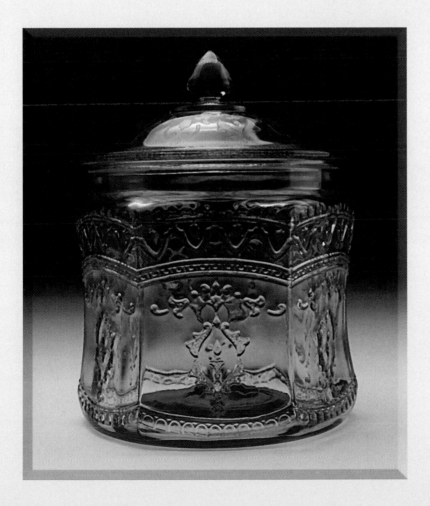

Patrician
Cookie jar, green,
Federal Glass Co.
$695.00.

"Peacock Reverse"
Vase, black, 10",
Paden City Glass Co.
$295.00.

"Peacock Reverse"
Octagonal plate, pink, 8½",
Paden City Glass Co.
$65.00.

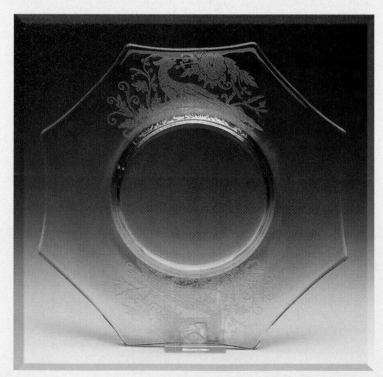

"Peacock Reverse"
Round candy dish, green, 6",
Paden City Glass Co.
$225.00.

"Peacock & Wild Rose"
Elliptical vase, black, 8¼",
Paden City Glass Co.
$395.00.

"Peacock & Wild Rose"
Console bowl, amber satinized, 11",
Paden City Glass Co.
$125.00.

"Peacock & Wild Rose"
Vase, cobalt, 10¼", Paden City Glass Co.
$395.00.

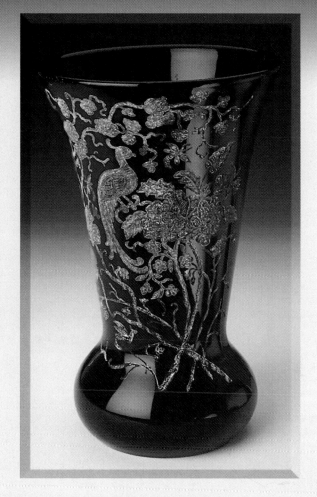

"Peacock & Wild Rose"
Vase, ebony, 10¼", Paden City Glass Co.
$395.00.

"Peacock & Wild Rose"
Console bowl, blue, 11",
Paden City Glass Co.
$495.00.

"Peacock & Wild Rose"
Fan vase, pink, 8½",
Paden City Glass Co.
$395.00.

"Peacock & Wild Rose"
Individual green sugar and creamer, large pink sugar,
Paden City Glass Co.
Green sugar and creamer, $75.00 each; large pink sugar, $55.00.

Petalware, "Monax Florette"
Decorated soup, 7",
MacBeth-Evans Glass Co.
$100.00.

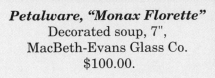

**Petalware,
"Mountain Flower"**
Pitchers and tumblers,
MacBeth-Evans Glass Co.
Crystal pitcher, $300.00;
frosted pitcher, $200.00;
tumblers, $50.00 each.

"Philbe," Fire-King
Candy jar, blue, 4",
Anchor Hocking Glass Co.
$795.00.

"Philbe," Fire-King
Cup and saucer, blue,
Anchor Hocking Glass Co.
$275.00.

"Philbe," Fire-King
Water goblet, blue, 7¼", 9 ounce,
Anchor Hocking Glass Co.
$235.00.

"Philbe," Fire-King
Juice pitcher, blue, 6", 36 ounce,
Anchor Hocking Glass Co.
$895.00.

"Philbe," Fire-King
Water tumbler, blue, 4", 9 ounce,
Anchor Hocking Glass Co.
$135.00.

"Philbe," Fire-King
Cookie jar, blue, Anchor Hocking Glass Co.
$1,500.00.

"Philbe," Fire-King
Platter, blue, Anchor
Hocking Glass Co.
$295.00.

Pillar Optic
Footed tumbler, red,
Anchor Hocking Glass Co.
$55.00.

Plantation
Epergne candleholder, crystal, 5",
A. H. Heisey & Co.
$150.00.

Plantation
Candy dish, crystal, 5", A. H. Heisey & Co.
$750.00.

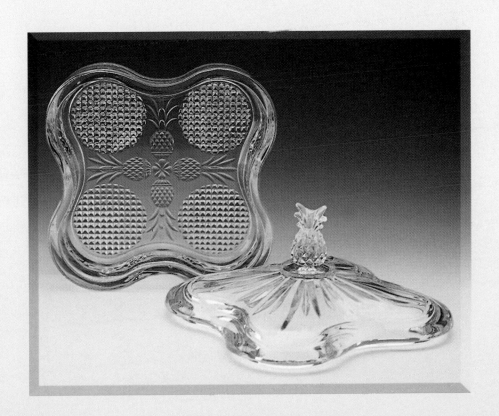

Plantation
Divided relish, crystal, A. H. Heisey & Co.
$1,000.00.

Plantation
Coupe plate, crystal,
A. H. Heisey & Co.
$500.00.

Portia
#1341 mushroom cordial, amber,
Cambridge Glass Co.
$125.00.

Portia
#3126 cordial, amber,
Cambridge Glass Co.
$300.00.

Portia
#3035 cocktail, gold-encrusted Carmen,
Cambridge Glass Co.
$450.00.

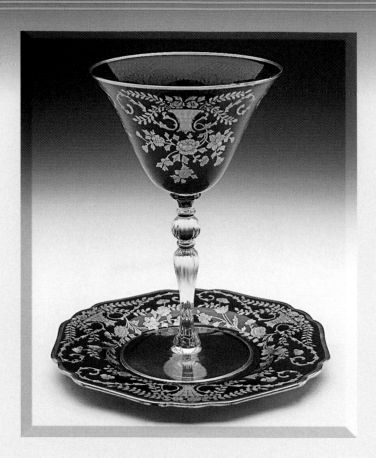

Portia
Sherbet and sherbet plate, gold-encrusted
Carmen, Cambridge Glass Co.
Sherbet, $400.00; plate, $250.00.

Portia
Vase, gold-encrusted Carmen,
Cambridge Glass Co.
$1,500.00.

Portia
Cigarette or card holder, gold-encrusted
Carmen, Cambridge Glass Co.
$1,250.00.

Portia
#3400/114 pitcher, Crown Tuscan
with gold, 80 ounce,
Cambridge Glass Co.
$1,250.00.

Portia
Cornucopia vases, Crown
Tuscan with gold,
Cambridge Glass Co.
$295.00 each.

Portia
#1237 vase, Crown Tuscan
with gold, 9",
Cambridge Glass Co.
$250.00.

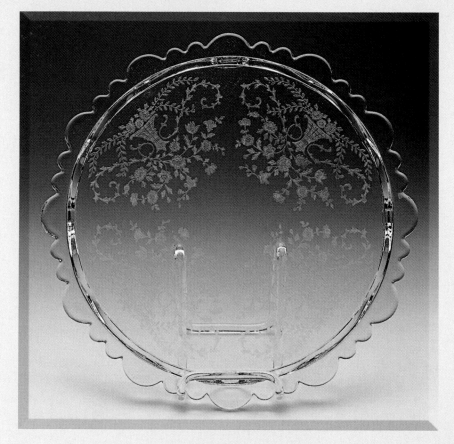

Portia
#170 Martha cake plate, crystal, 13", Cambridge Glass Co.
$200.00.

Portia
#3500/78 ram's head candy box and cover, crystal, 6",
Cambridge Glass Co.
$250.00.

Portia
#3400/69 after dinner cup and saucer,
crystal with gold decoration, 6",
Cambridge Glass Co.
$125.00.

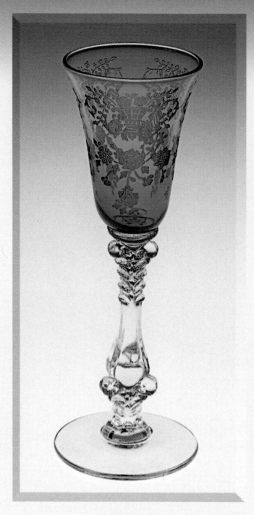

Portia
#3400/54 cup, Emerald green (dark),
Cambridge Glass Co.
$85.00.

Portia
#3121 cordial, Emerald green (dark),
Cambridge Glass Co.
$395.00.

Portia
#3400/1180 two-handled
bonbon, Heatherbloom,
5¼", Cambridge Glass Co.
$85.00.

Portia
Pitcher, Heatherbloom,
Cambridge Glass Co.
$1,250.00.

Portia
Tumbler, Heatherbloom,
Cambridge Glass Co.
$125.00.

Primrose, Fire-King
Gravy pitcher,
Anchor Hocking Glass Co.
$325.00.

Primrose, Fire-King
Vintage footed fruit bowl,
Anchor Hocking Glass Co.
$175.00.

Primrose, Fire-King
Meat platter,
Anchor Hocking Glass Co.
$225.00.

Primrose, Fire-King
Napco vase, Anchor Hocking Glass Co.
$175.00.

Princess
Three-part, three-footed relish, blue, 8¾",
Anchor Hocking Glass Co.
$1,250.00.

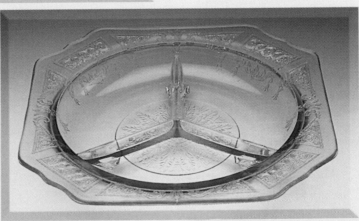

Princess
Non-stemmed sherbet, green,
Anchor Hocking Glass Co.
$125.00.

Princess
Dinner plate, blue, 9½", Anchor Hocking Glass Co.
$200.00.

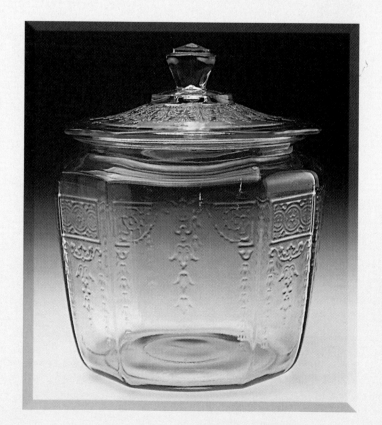

Princess
Cookie jar, blue, Anchor Hocking Glass Co.
$895.00.

Princess
Footed pitcher and
tumbler, green,
Anchor Hocking Glass Co.
Pitcher, $595.00;
tumbler, $65.00.

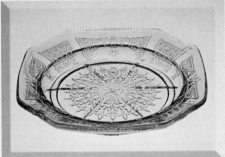

Princess
Coaster, yellow,
Anchor Hocking Glass Co.
$125.00.

Princess
Square, three-footed relish,
pink, 8¾",
Anchor Hocking Glass Co.
$895.00.

Princess
Soup or undivided relish,
yellow, 7½",
Anchor Hocking Glass Co.
$350.00.

Princess
Juice pitcher, yellow,
Anchor Hocking Glass Co.
$895.00.

Queen Anne
#1509 three-footed individual
candlestick, crystal, 3",
A. H. Heisey & Co.
$75.00.

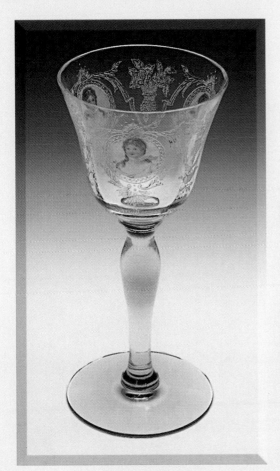

Queen Louise
Cocktail, 3 ounce,
Morgantown Glass Works.
$400.00.

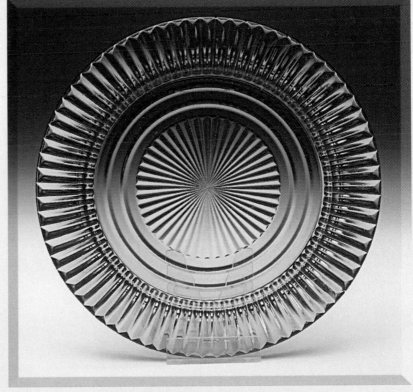

Queen Mary
Salad plate, blue, Anchor Hockey Glass Co.
$75.00.

Queen Mary
Footed creamer and sugar, crystal (above) and pink (below),
Anchor Hocking Glass Co.
Crystal creamer and sugar, $25.00 each; pink creamer and sugar, $65.00 each.

Queen Mary
Three-footed bowl, pink,
Anchor Hocking Glass Co.
$75.00.

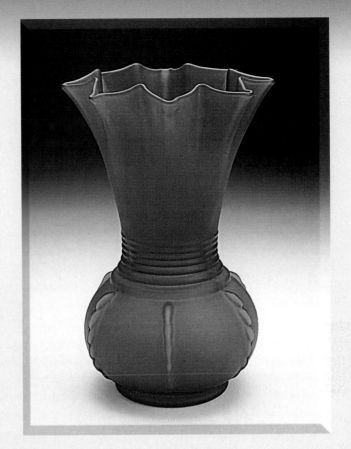

Radiance
Satinized vase, amethyst, 10",
New Martinsville Glass Co.
$140.00.

Radiance
Satinized vase, black, 10",
New Martinsville Glass Co.
$140.00.

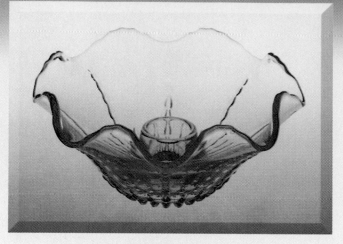

Radiance
Cup and saucer, pink,
New Martinsville Glass Co.
$75.00.

Radiance
Ruffled candleholder, ice blue, 6",
New Martinsville Glass Co.
$85.00.

Radiance
Vase, pink, 10",
New Martinsville Glass Co.
$175.00.

Radiance
Ball candleholder, red, 5",
New Martinsville Glass Co.
$90.00.

Radiance
Comport, ruby, 5¼" x 6½",
New Martinsville Glass Co.
$85.00.

Radiance
Candleholder with bobeches, red, 8",
New Martinsville Glass Co.
$175.00.

Radiance
Punch set, ruby, New Martinsville Glass Co.
$595.00.

Ridgeleigh
Tumbler, crystal, 6",
A.H. Heisey & Co.
$135.00.

Radiance
Candleholder with bobeche, blue,
New Martinsville Co.
$295.00.

Ridgeleigh
Oval hors d'oeuvres plate, crystal,
A.H. Heisey & Co.
$650.00.

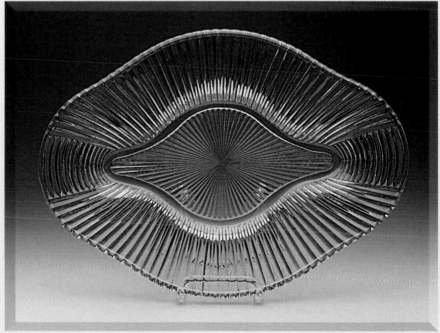

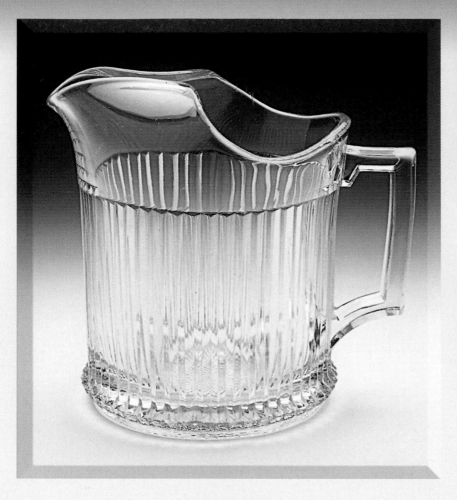

Ridgeleigh
Pitcher, crystal, ½ gallon, A.H. Heisey & Co.
$350.00.

Ring
Goblet, yellow, 7¼",
Hocking Glass Co.
$95.00.

Ring
Cup and saucer, blue,
Hocking Glass Co.
$75.00.

Rock Crystal
Footed center bowl,
amber, 12½",
McKee Glass Co.
$125.00.

Rock Crystal
Cheese dish, crystal, butter lid for comparison (right), McKee Glass Co.
Cheese dish, $595.00; butter lid, $225.00.

Rock Crystal
Footed centerpiece bowl, cobalt, 12½", McKee Glass Co.
$325.00.

Rock Crystal
Satinized candlestick, jap blue,
8", McKee Glass Co.
$125.00.

Rock Crystal
Center-handled bowl, red, 8½", McKee Glass Co.
$300.00.

Rock Crystal
Syrup pitcher, red, McKee Glass Co.
$995.00.

Rosalie
#731 vase, Emerald green with spiral optic,
10", Cambridge Glass Co.
$250.00.

Rosalie
#731 bowl, Peach-Blo, 14",
Cambridge Glass Co.
$295.00.

Rosalie
#731 goblet, Topaz bowl with
Willow blue stem, 9 ounce
Cambridge Glass Co.
$125.00.

Rosalie
#731 wine goblet, Carmen,
Cambridge Glass Co.
$100.00.

Rosalie
#731 sherbet with liner, Bluebell,
Cambridge Glass Co.
Sherbet, $55.00; liner, $20.00.

Rosalie
#731 enamel fill water goblet,
Emerald green,
Cambridge Glass Co.
$100.00.

Rosalie
#731 candy with lid, Emerald green,
Cambridge Glass Co.
$200.00.

Rosalie
#519 shot glass, #731 Peach-Blo,
1¾ ounce, 2⅞" high,
Cambridge Glass Co.
$100.00.

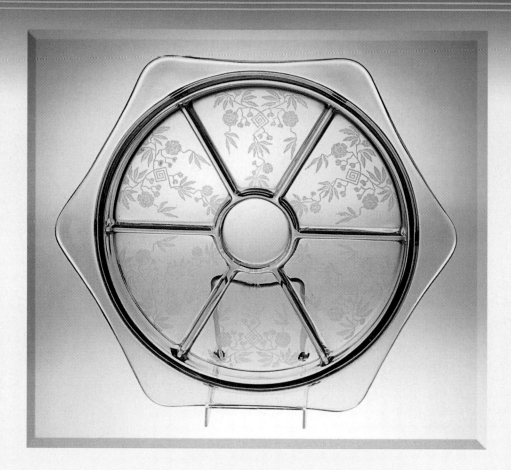

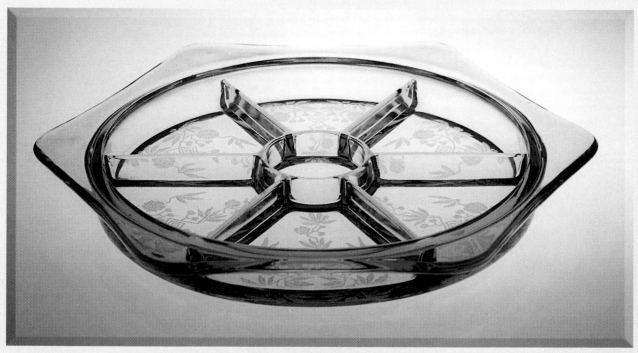

Rosalie
Seven-part relish, Emerald green,
Cambridge Glass Co.
$225.00.

Rose
Epergne bowl with epergne vase,
crystal, 9½",
A.H. Heisey & Co.
$450.00.

Rose
Epergne bowl with etched
Rose epergnette, 6"
deep candle, 9½",
A.H. Heisey & Co.
$1,350.00.

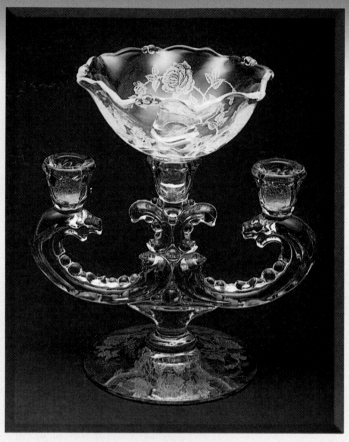

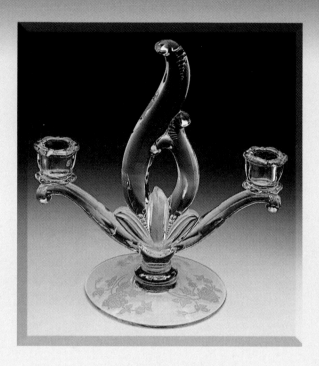

Rose
Flame candleholder, A.H. Heisey & Co.
$450.00.

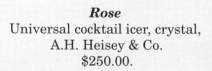

Rose
Epergnette, crystal, A.H. Heisey & Co.
$1,250.00.

Rose
Universal cocktail icer, crystal,
A.H. Heisey & Co.
$250.00.

Rosepoint
#3500 cordial, gold-encrusted Carmen,
1 ounce, Cambridge Glass Co.
$1,000.00.

Rosepoint
#3104 cocktail, crystal, 3½ ounce,
Cambridge Glass Co.
$600.00.

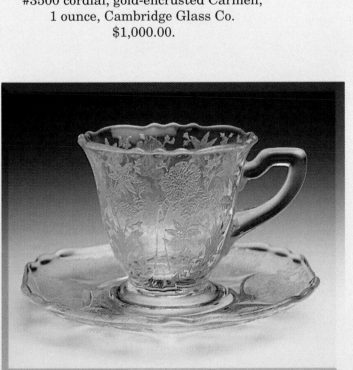

Rosepoint
After dinner cup and saucer, crystal,
Cambridge Glass Co.
$450.00.

Rosepoint
#3500 wine, gold-
encrusted Carmen,
Cambridge Glass Co.
$800.00.

Rosepoint
Tumbler, gold-encrusted
amber, Cambridge Glass Co.
$275.00.

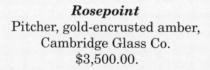

Rosepoint
Pitcher, gold-encrusted amber,
Cambridge Glass Co.
$3,500.00.

Rosepoint
Sugar, amber, Cambridge Glass Co.
$250.00.

Rosepoint
Ice bucket, amber, Cambridge Glass Co.
$1,750.00.

Rosepoint
Vase, Crown Tuscan with gold,
Cambridge Glass Co.
$2,000.00.

Rosepoint
Pitcher, gold-encrusted Carmen,
Cambridge Glass Co.
$8,500.00.

Rosepoint
Console bowl, Ebony with gold, 12",
Cambridge Glass Co.
$1,800.00.

Rosepoint
#1055 Weiss beer goblet, crystal with
gold, 32 ounce Cambridge Glass Co.
$1,500.00.

Rosepoint
Pressed stem cordial, cobalt,
Cambridge Glass Co.
$225.00.

Rosepoint
Pristine blown torte plate, crystal,
14", Cambridge Glass Co.
$500.00.

Rosepoint
#1470 ball shaker with Ebony base, crystal,
Cambridge Glass Co.
$100.00.

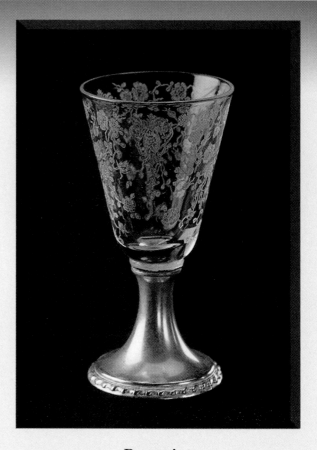

Rosepoint
#3106 cordial with Wallace sterling base,
crystal, Cambridge Glass Co.
$395.00.

Rosepoint
#222 three-part bowl, 10½
ounce, Cambridge Glass Co.
$350.00.

Rosepoint
#3400/77 shakers with Ebony tops, crystal,
Cambridge Glass Co.
$100.00 each.

Rosepoint
Cordial pressed with etched top,
crystal, Cambridge Glass Co.
$1,000.00.

Rosepoint
#498, 2 ounce bar
tumbler, #321, 2 ounce
sham to 1½ ounce bar
tumbler, crystal,
Cambridge Glass Co.
tumbler, $150.00;
sham, $175.00.

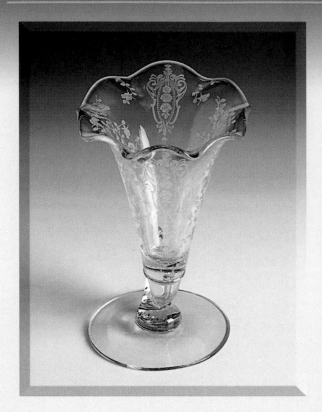

Rosepoint
Ruffled top cornucopia vase, crystal, Cambridge Glass Co.
$400.00.

Rosepoint
Vase, gold-encrusted Ebony, 11",
Cambridge Glass Co.
$1,250.00.

Rosepoint
Ball shaker with Wallace sterling base, crystal,
Cambridge Glass Co.
$75.00.

Rosepoint
Pressed water goblet with etched bowl,
Cambridge Glass Co.
$750.00.

Rosepoint
#944 sugar and
creamer, crystal,
Cambridge Glass Co.
Sugar, $150.00;
creamer, $175.00.

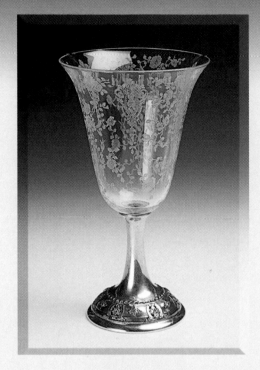

Rosepoint
Goblet with Wallace sterling
base, crystal,
Cambridge Glass Co.
$800.00.

Rosepoint
Pristine cocktail, crystal, 3½",
Cambridge Glass Co.
$450.00.

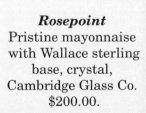

Rosepoint
Pristine mayonnaise
with Wallace sterling
base, crystal,
Cambridge Glass Co.
$200.00.

Rosepoint
#300 three-footed candy, gold-encrusted Ebony,
7", Cambridge Glass Co.
$2,500.00.

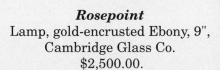

Rosepoint
#3750 footed iced tea tumbler,
crystal with gold, 12 ounce, although
Rosepoint, this was made at Imperial.
$125.00.

Rosepoint
Lamp, gold-encrusted Ebony, 9",
Cambridge Glass Co.
$2,500.00.

Rosepoint
Statuesque claret (left), statuesque goblet
(right), crystal with gold, Cambridge Glass Co.
Claret, $3,200.00; Goblet, $4,500.00.

Rosepoint
#278 vase, gold-encursted
Ebony (rare color), 11",
Cambridge Glass Co.
$1,500.00.

Royal Lace
Nut bowl, green, Hazel Atlas Glass Co.
$600.00.

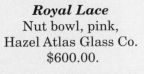

Royal Lace
Nut bowl, cobalt blue,
Hazel Atlas Glass Co.
$1,800.00.

Royal Lace
Nut bowl, pink,
Hazel Atlas Glass Co.
$600.00.

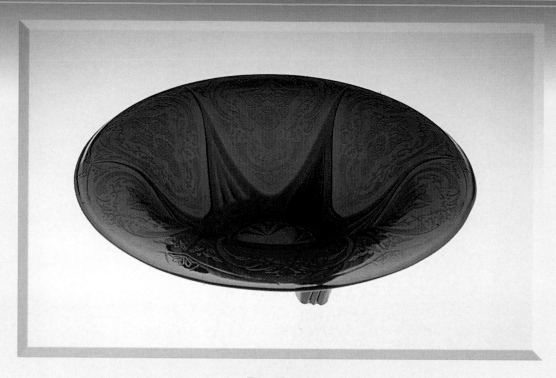

Royal Lace
Rolled edge console bowl, amethyst, Hazel Atlas Glass Co.
$1,000.00.

Royal Lace
Sugar bowl, iridescent,
Hazel Atlas Glass Co.
$50.00.

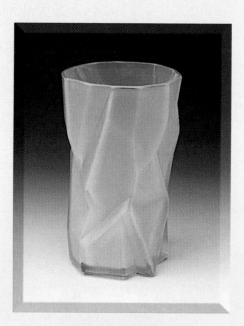

Ruba Rombic
Flat tumbler, Jade, 12 ounce,
Consolidated Lamp & Glass Co.
$185.00.

Ruba Rombic
Creamer, Lilac,
Consolidated Lamp & Glass Co.
$250.00.

Ruba Rombic
Sugar, Jungle Green,
Consolidated Lamp & Glass Co.
$250.00.

Ruba Rombic
Vase, Ebony, 9",
Consolidated Lamp & Glass Co.
$1,800.00.

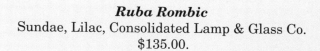

Ruba Rombic
Ashtray, Lilac, 3½",
Consolidated Lamp & Glass Co.
$600.00.

Ruba Rombic
Sundae, Lilac, Consolidated Lamp & Glass Co.
$135.00.

Ruba Rombic
Almond, Smokey Topaz, 3",
Consolidated Lamp & Glass Co.
$300.00.

Ruba Rombic
Footed tumbler, Smokey Topaz,
15 ounce, 7",
Consolidated Lamp & Glass Co.
$375.00.

"S" Pattern
Straight-sided tumbler,
crystal, 10 ounce,
MacBeth-Evans Glass Co.
$25.00.

"S" Pattern
Pitcher and tumbler, green,
MacBeth-Evans Glass Co.
Pitcher, $595.00; tumbler, $55.00.

Sandwich
Scalloped bowl, crystal, 7½", Anchor Hocking Glass Co.
$135.00.

Sandwich
Opalescent bowl, pink, Anchor Hocking Glass Co.
$100.00.

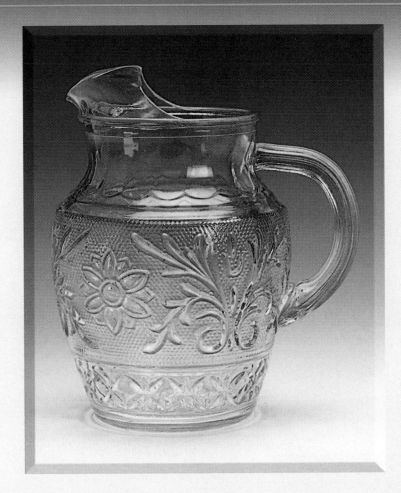

Sandwich
Juice pitcher, pink, 6",
Anchor Hocking Glass Co.
$395.00.

Saturn
Marmalade (left), and paddle (right), Zircon, A.H. Heisey & Co.
$900.00.

Saturn
Two-lite candlestick, Zircon, A.H. Heisey & Co.
$650.00.

Scottie Dog
Powder jar, transparent blue,
Akro Agate Co.
$595.00.

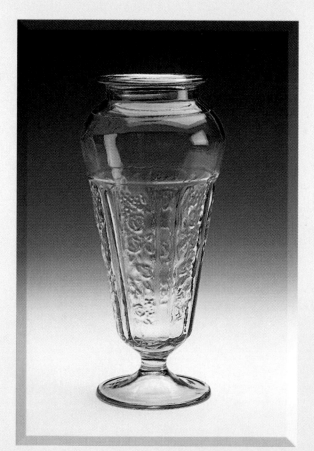

Sharon
Footed vase, pink, Federal Glass Co.
$1,500.00.

"Sheaves of Wheat"
Cup, yellow, Anchor Hocking Glass Co.
$150.00.

Shell Pink
Advertising ashtray, Jeannette Glass Co.
$350.00.

Shell Pink
Bird candleholder, Jeannette Glass Co.
$400.00 pair.

Shell Pink
Duck powder jar, Jeannette Glass Co.
$350.00.

Silver Crest
Footed shaker, white,
Fenton Glass Co.
$125.00.

Silver Crest
Shaker, white, Fenton Glass Co.
$75.00.

Silver Crest
Sugar and creamer, white with crystal trim,
Fenton Glass Co.
$135.00 each.

Square
Tumbler with ruffled top, crystal,
Cambridge Glass Co.
$150.00.

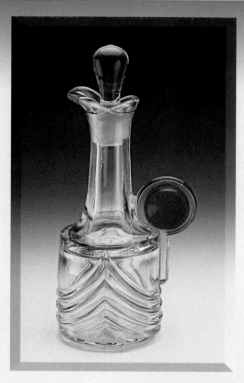

Stanhope
Cruet, crystal, A.H. Heisey & Co.
$350.00.

Star
Butter dish, crystal,
Federal Glass Co.
$100.00.

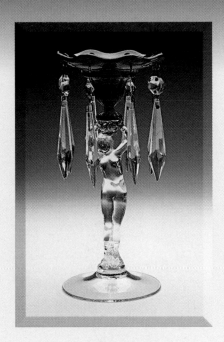

Statuesque
#3011 candlestick, Carmen,
Cambridge Glass Co.
$850.00.

Statuesque
#3011 blown covered comport,
Carmen, Cambridge Glass Co.
$2,000.00.

Statuesque
#3011 bud vase, Amethyst,
Cambridge Glass Co.
$1,500.00.

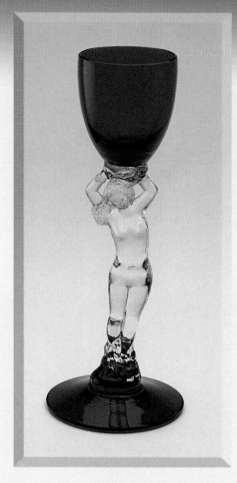

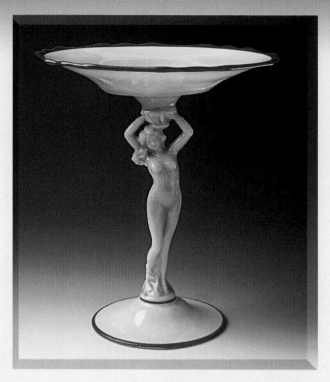

Statuesque
#3011 comport, Crown Tuscan with rare
red trim,
Cambridge Glass Co.
$2,000.00.

Statuesque
#3011 bowl, Carmen bowl and
Royal blue foot,
Cambridge Glass Co.Only known
example of this color combination.
$5,000.00.

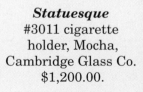

Statuesque
#3011 cigarette
holder, Mocha,
Cambridge Glass Co.
$1,200.00.

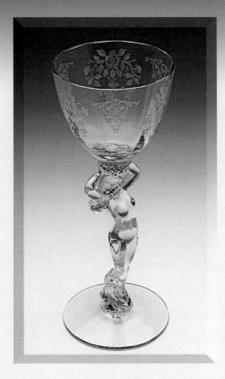

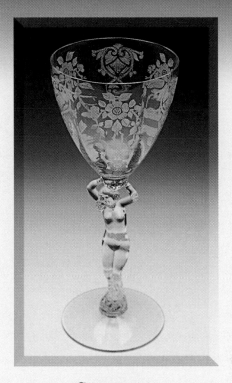

Statuesque
#3011 claret with Apple
Blossom etch, Heatherbloom,
Cambridge Glass Co.
$2,000.00.

Statuesque
#3011 water goblet with Apple
Blossom etch, Heatherbloom,
Cambridge Glass Co.
$2,400.00.

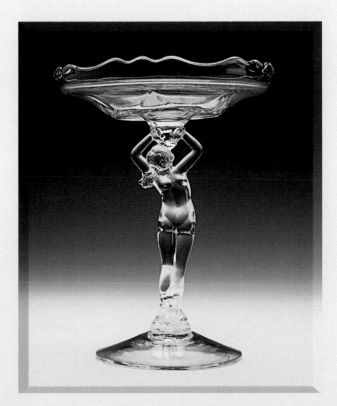

Statuesque
#3011 comport, Moonlight blue,
Cambridge Glass Co.
$1,200.00.

Statuesque
#3011 cocktail, Smoke crackle,
Cambridge Glass Co.
$750.00.

Statuesque
#3011 sweetmeat, Royal blue,
Cambridge Glass Co.
$1,500.00.

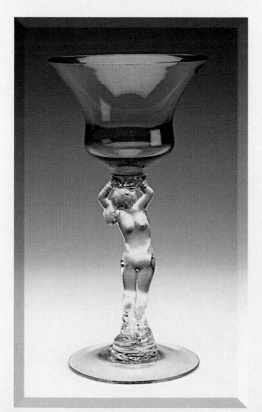

Statuesque
#3011 tulip cocktail, Emerald green (dark),
Cambridge Glass Co.
$600.00.

Sunflower
Saucer, cup, and plate, Delphite, Jeannette Glass Co.
Saucer, $25.00; plate, $100.00; cup, $75.00.

Sunflower
Coaster, green, Jeannette Glass Co.
$250.00.

Sunflower
Tab-handled bowl,
Delphite blue, 6",
Jeannette Glass Co.
$100.00.

Sunflower
Salad plate, pink, 8",
Jeannette Glass Co.
$50.00.

**Sunrise Medallion,
"Dancing Girl"**
Tumbler, blue, 4 ounce, 2⅞",
Morgantown Glass Works.
$150.00.

**Sunrise Medallion,
"Dancing Girl"**
Creamer and sugar, blue, Morgantown Glass Works.
Sugar, $300.00; Creamer, $325.00.

**Sunrise Medallion,
"Dancing Girl"**
Sugar bowl, green,
Morgantown Glass Works.
$250.00.

**Sunrise Medallion,
"Dancing Girl"**
Goblet, crystal with opal stem,
Morgantown Glass Works.
$150.00.

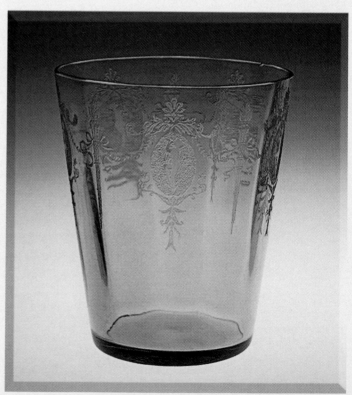

**Sunrise Medallion,
"Dancing Girl"**
Vase, pink, 6", Morgantown Glass Works.
$450.00.

**Sunrise Medallion,
"Dancing Girl"**
Sugar bowl, pink,
Morgantown Glass Works.
$250.00.

Swirl
Footed pitcher, Ultramarine, 48 ounce,
Jeannette Glass Co.
$2,250.00.

Tea Room
Ruffled vase, amber, 6½",
Indiana Glass Co.
$350.00.

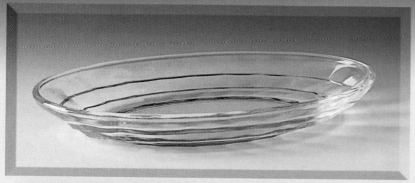

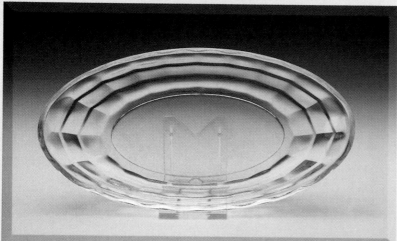

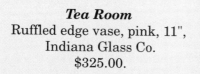

Tea Room
Flat banana split, crystal,
Indiana Glass Co.
$95.00.

Tea Room
Ruffled edge vase, pink, 11",
Indiana Glass Co.
$325.00.

Trojan
#2439 decanter, topaz, Fostoria Glass Co.
$1,790.00.

Tulip
Decanter with Tulip stopper, blue,
Dell Glass Co.
$495.00.

Twist
Cocktail shaker, Moongleam,
A.H. Heisey & Co.
$425.00.

Valencia
#3500/30 ashtray, crystal, 4", Cambridge Glass Co.
$125.00.

Valencia
#3500/16 footed console bowl, Peach-Blo, 11", Cambridge Glass Co.
$250.00.

Valencia
#3500/31candlestick, Peach-Blo, 6",
Cambridge Glass Co.
$200.00.

Versailles
#2439 decanter, Azure,
Fostoria Glass Co.
$2,795.00.

Victorian
Jug, crystal, 54 ounce,
A.H. Heisey & Co.
$350.00.

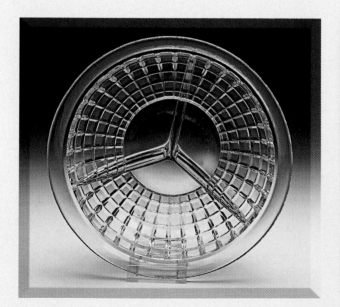 

Victorian
Three-part bowl, crystal, A.H. Heisey & Co.
$275.00.

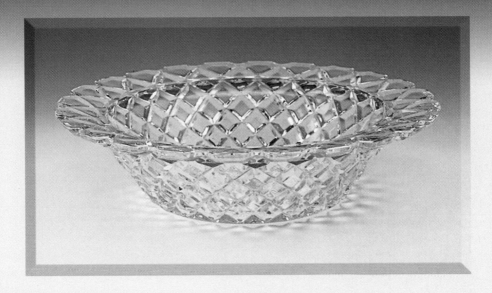

Waterford
Bowl, crystal, 7¾ x 2" high, Hocking Glass Co.
$40.00.

Waterford
Water goblet and juice, "Miss America
style," pink, Hocking Glass Co.
$125.00.

Waverly
#1519 candlestick, crystal, 4½",
A.H. Heisey & Co.
$95.00.

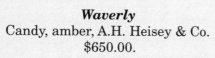

Waverly
Candy, amber, A.H. Heisey & Co.
$650.00.

Waverly
Lion cover trinket box, crystal,
A.H. Heisey & Co.
$650.00.

Wildflower
#1238 vase, Emerald green (dark), 12",
Cambridge Glass Co.
$350.00.

Wildflower
#3400/35 two-handled plate, gold-encrusted amber, 11",
Cambridge Glass Co.
$175.00.

Wildflower
#3400/647 double candle, amber with gold,
Cambridge Glass Co.
$150.00.

Wildflower
#119 basket, crystal, 7",
Cambridge Glass Co.
$400.00.

Wildflower
#3116 cut water goblet, crystal,
Cambridge Glass Co.
$125.00.

Wildflower
#3400/69 after dinner cup and saucer,
crystal, Cambridge Glass Co.
$200.00.

Wildflower
Martha punch bowl set, crystal, Cambridge Glass Co.
$4,500.00.

Wildflower
#648/119 candelabrum, Ebony with gold
decoration, 6", Cambridge Glass Co.
$500.00.

Wildflower
Center-handle server, Peach-Blo,
Cambridge Glass Co.
$250.00.

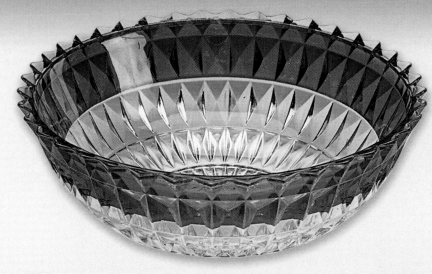

Windsor
Pointed edge bowl, crystal, flashed
red, 8", Jeannette Glass Co.
$45.00.

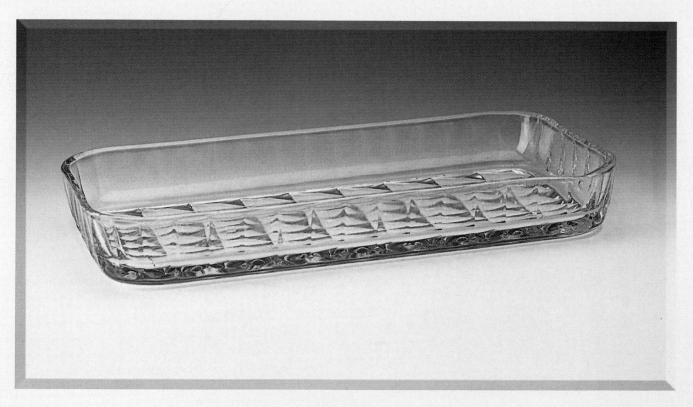

Windsor
Tray without handles, pink, 4⅛" x 9", Jeannette Glass Co.
$60.00.

Windsor
Three-part platter, pink, 11½", Jeannette Glass Co.
$250.00.

Windsor
Tab-handled berry bowl, pink, Jeannette Glass Co.
$95.00.

Windsor
Pitcher and tumbler, red,
Jeannette Glass Co.
Pitcher, $450.00; tumbler, $55.00.

Windsor
Creamer, transparent blue,
Jeannette Glass Co.
$75.00.

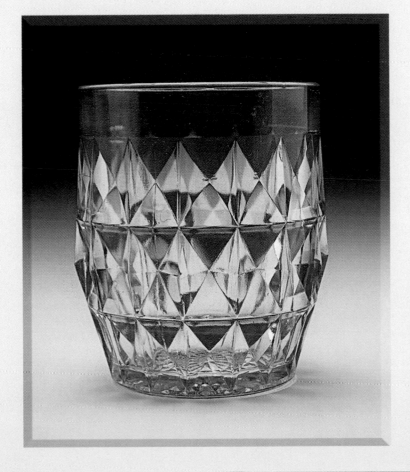

Windsor
Tumbler, transparent blue,
Jeannette Glass Co.
$85.00.

Windsor
Powder jar, yellow,
Jeannette Glass Co.
$295.00.

Yeoman
Sherbet, amber, Heisey Glass Co.
$125.00.

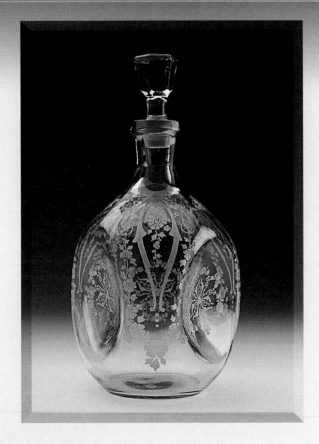

Diane
Pinch decanter, Peach-Blo,
Cambridge Glass Co.
$495.00.

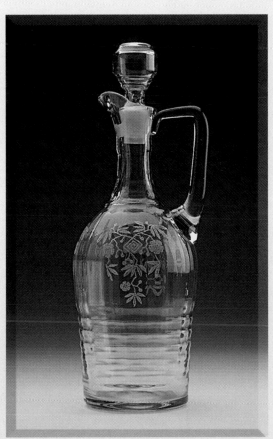

Rosalie
Handled decanter, Willow
blue, Cambridge Glass Co.
$495.00.

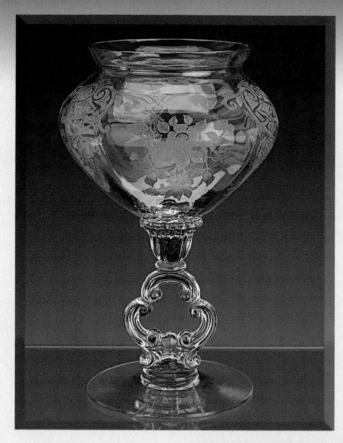

Apple Blossom
Keyhole vase, Peach-Blo,
Cambridge Glass Co.
$450.00.

Portia
Samovar and shot glass, 2 ounce, crystal,
Cambridge Glass Co.
Samovar, $495.00; shot glass, $65.00.

Collectible GLASSWARE from the 40s, 50s, and 60s, 7th Edition *Gene Florence*

Gene Florence, the foremost authority on glassware, has produced a revamped edition of *Collectible Glassware from the 40s, 50s, and 60s*. Covering collectible glassware made after the Depression era, this is the only book available that deals exclusively with the handmade and mass-produced glassware from this period. It is completely updated, featuring many original company catalog pages and 19 new patterns — making a total of 121 patterns from Anniversary to Yorktown, with many of the most popular Fire-King patterns in between. Each pattern is alphabetically listed, all known pieces in each pattern are described and priced, and gorgeous color photographs showcase both common and very rare pieces. Florence's descriptive text offers insights into and evaluations of each pattern's history, popularity, and value on today's exciting collectibles market. 2004 values.

Item #6325 • ISBN: 1-57432-351-2 • 8½ x 11 • 256 Pgs. • HB • $19.95

Collector's Encyclopedia of DEPRESSION GLASS, 16th Edition *Gene Florence*

Since the first edition of *Collector's Encyclopedia of Depression Glass* was released in 1972, it has been America's #1 bestselling glass book. Gene Florence now presents this completely revised 16th edition, with the previous 133 patterns and 15 additional patterns, to make this the most complete reference to date. With the assistance of several nationally known dealers, this book illustrates, as well as realistically prices, items in demand. Dealing primarily with the glass made from the 1920s through the end of the 1930s, this beautiful reference book contains stunning color photographs, vintage catalog pages, updated values, and a special section on reissues and fakes. This dependable information comes from years of research, experience, fellow dealers and collectors, and millions of miles of travel by full-time glass dealer Gene Florence, America's leading glassware authority. 2004 values.

Item #6327 • ISBN: 1-57432-353-9 • 8½ x 11 • 256 Pgs. • HB • $19.95

VERY RARE GLASSWARE of the Depression Years *Gene Florence*

These popular books by Gene Florence will help the collector spot those rare and valuable pieces of Depression glass that may come around once in a lifetime. Florence is America's leading glassware authority, and these books are considered required reading. They are jam-packed with full-color photos and information featuring rare examples of Depression items, as well as elegant and kitchen items. There are absolutely no repeats in these books. Both are "musts" for anyone interested in Depression glass — they are necessary tools to help spot those very rare pieces and let you know what they are actually worth.

Fifth Series • Item #4732 • ISBN: 0-89145-739-9
8½ x 11 • 192 Pgs. • HB • 1997 values • $24.95
Sixth Series • Item #5170 • ISBN: 1-57432-095-5
8½ x 11 • 176 Pgs. • HB • 1999 values • $24.95

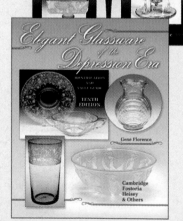

ELEGANT GLASSWARE of the Depression Era, 10th Edition *Gene Florence*

This new edition holds hundreds of new photographs, listings, and updated values. This book features the handmade and acid-etched glassware that was sold in department and jewelry stores from the Depression era through the 1950s, not the dimestore and give-away glass known as Depression glass. As always, glassware authority Gene Florence has added many new discoveries, 10 additional patterns, and re-photographed many items from the previous books. Large group settings are included for each of the more than 100 patterns, as well as close-ups to show pattern details. The famous glassmakers presented include Fenton, Cambridge, Heisey, Tiffin, Imperial, Duncan & Miller, U.S. Glass, and Paden City. Florence provides a list of all known pieces, with colors and measurements, along with 2003 values.

Item #6125 • ISBN: 1-57432-298-2 • 8½ x 11 • 240 Pgs. • HB • $24.95

KITCHEN GLASSWARE of the Depression Years, 6th Edition
Gene Florence

This exciting new edition of our bestselling *Kitchen Glassware of the Depression Years* is undeniably the definitive reference on the subject. More than 5,000 items are showcased in beautiful professional color photographs with descriptions and values. Many new finds and exceptionally rare pieces have been added. The highly collectible glass from the Depression era through the 1960s fills its pages, in addition to the ever-popular Fire-King and Pyrex glassware. This comprehensive encyclopedia provides an easy-to-use format, showing items by color, shape, or pattern. The collector will enjoy the pages of glass, from colorful juice reamers, shakers, rare and unusual glass knives, to the mixing bowls and baking dishes we still find in our kitchen cupboards. 2003 values.

Item #5827 • ISBN: 1-57432-220-6 • 8½ x 11 • 272 Pgs. • HB • $24.95

Anchor Hocking's FIRE-KING & More, 2nd Edition
Gene Florence

From the 1930s to the 1960s Anchor Hocking Glass Corp. of Lancaster, Ohio, produced an extensive line of glassware called Fire-King. Their lines included not only dinnerware but also a plethora of glass kitchen items — reamers, measuring cups, mixing bowls, mugs, and more. This is the essential collectors' reference to this massive line of glassware. Loaded with hundreds of new full-color photos, vintage catalog pages, company materials, facts, information, and values, this book has everything collectors expect from Gene Florence. 2002 values.

Item #5602 • ISBN: 1-57432-164-1 • 8½ x 11 • 224 Pgs. • HB • $24.95

Glass CANDLESTICKS of the Depression Era
Gene Florence

Florence has compiled this book to help identify the candlestick patterns made during the Depression era. More than 500 different candlesticks are shown in full-color photographs. The book is arranged according to color: amber, black, blue, crystal, green, iridescent, multicolor, pink, purple, red, smoke, white, and yellow. Many famous glassmakers are represented, such as Heisey, Cambridge, Fostoria, and Tiffin. The descriptive text for each candleholder includes pattern, maker, color, height, and current collector value. A helpful index and bibliography are also provided. 2000 values.

Item #5354 • ISBN: 1-57432-136-6 • 8½ x 11 • 176 Pgs. • HB • $24.95

Florence's Glassware PATTERN IDENTIFICATION Guide
Gene Florence

Florence's Glassware Pattern Identification Guides are great companions for his other glassware books. Volume I includes every pattern featured in his *Collector's Encyclopedia of Depression Glass, Collectible Glassware from the 40s, 50s, and 60s,* and *Collector's Encyclopedia of Elegant Glassware,* as well as many more — nearly 400 patterns in all. Volume II holds nearly 500 patterns, with no repeats from Volume I. Volume III also showcases nearly 500 patterns with no repeats from the previous volumes. Carefully planned close-up photographs of representative pieces for every pattern show great detail to make identification easy. With every pattern, Florence provides the names, the companies which made the glass, dates of production, and even colors available. These guides are ideal references for novice and seasoned glass collectors and dealers, and great resources for years to come. No values.

Vol. I • Item #5042 • ISBN: 1-57432-045-9 • 8½ x 11 • 176 Pgs. • PB • $18.95
Vol. II • Item #5615 • ISBN: 1-57432-177-3 • 8½ x 11 • 208 Pgs. • PB • $19.95
Vol. III • Item #6142 • ISBN: 1-57432-315-6 • 8½ x 11 • 272 Pgs. • PB • $19.95

Pocket Guide to DEPRESSION GLASS & More, 13th Edition
Gene Florence

Gene Florence has completely revised his *Pocket Guide to Depression Glass* with over 4,000 values updated to reflect the ever-changing market. Many of the photographs have been reshot to improve the quality and add new finds. There are a total of 119 new photos for this edition, including 29 additional patterns that have not appeared in previous editions. These gorgeous photographs show great detail, and the listings of the patterns and their available pieces make identification simple. There is even a section on re-issues and the numerous fakes flooding the market. This is the perfect book to take with you on your searches through shops and flea markets and is the ideal companion to Florence's comprehensive *Collector's Encyclopedia of Depression Glass.* 2003 values.

Item #6136 • ISBN: 1-57432-309-1 • 5½ x 8½ • 224 Pgs. • PB • $12.95

Schroeder's ANTIQUES Price Guide

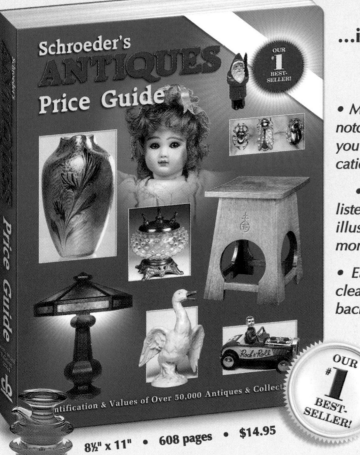

Schroeder's ANTIQUES Price Guide

OUR #1 BEST-SELLER!

8½" x 11" • 608 pages • $14.95

...is the #1 bestselling antiques & collectibles value guide on the market today, and here's why...

• More than 400 advisors, well-known dealers, and top-notch collectors work together with our editors to bring you accurate information regarding pricing and identification.

• More than 50,000 items in over 500 categories are listed along with hundreds of sharp original photos that illustrate not only the rare and unusual, but the common, popular collectibles as well.

• Each large close-up shot shows important details clearly. Every subject is represented with histories and background information, a feature not found in any of our competitors' publications.

• Our editors keep abreast of newly developing trends, often adding several new categories a year as the need arises.

OUR #1 BEST-SELLER!

Without doubt, you'll find

Schroeder's Antiques Price Guide

the only one to buy for reliable information and values.

If it merits the interest of today's collector, you'll find it in *Schroeder's*. And you can feel confident that the information we publish is up-to-date and accurate. Our advisors thoroughly check each category to spot inconsistencies, listings that may not be entirely reflective of market dealings, and lines too vague to be of merit. Only the best of the lot remains for publication.

COLLECTOR BOOKS
P.O. Box 3009, Paducah, KY 42002–3009
www.collectorbooks.com